**THE UNAUTHORIZED
AUTOBIOGRAPHY**

I want to dedicate this book to Kay Dotrice, who passed away suddenly a couple of months before the writing of this book. Kay *played our nanny in* Cheech and Chong's The Corsican Brothers. *She was the darling wife of Roy "Evil Fuckaire" Dotrice. Kay was everyone's mum on the set, and she always had a beautiful smile and words of encouragement for us all. I saw Kay at a party just before she died and we talked. She was worried about Roy because he was "getting on," as she put it. When I lost my mom, I was in mourning for many years because you never really get over losing a mom. I will never get over losing Kay. You will always be tucked away in my heart, dear Kay, forever. We all miss you dearly.*

CONTENTS

PLEASE WELCOME CHEECH AND CHONG

The Forum, Los Angeles, 1973

The roar from the crowd was loud. Almost frightening. It sounded like there were sixteen thousand hungry animals screaming to be fed, and we were the food—well actually, the appetizers; the Rolling Stones were the main course. The sixteen thousand–plus fans were there to see the greatest druggie rock band in the world, and we were about to be introduced into their world for the first time as the added feature act, thanks to our record producer–manager Lou Adler, who knew everyone in the music business. At the time, he *was* the music business.

That sound of thousands of people clapping and cheering acts like a drug. Actually, the high is way better; it is a rush unequaled by any drug, illegal or otherwise, and the addiction can last a lifetime. It's the same rush that makes boxers risk life and limb by fighting way past their prime. That special sound of love and anticipation directed toward you, and only you, sends shivers up and down your spine. A glow comes over your body and all of your senses switch to automatic. Each moment becomes so huge, the flow of events is measured in microseconds, not minutes. And each second flows into the next so seamlessly that it's over before you know it. You leave the screaming crowd wringing wet with sweat, totally unaware of body pain, feeling only extreme bliss. All you feel at the time is the moment itself.

This is why actors, musicians, teachers, lawyers, athletes, and performers live for that moment. And we die a little when that moment is over because each time we give a performance, a little is left onstage that never comes home with us again. A piece of our soul is locked in time to be brought back only in memories and, eventually, buried forever. And the first moment is the one you will always remember.

The drug that produces this electric effect is produced naturally by your body. It is the fight-or-flight drug, and it gives the body superhuman strength whenever it is threatened or stimulated by some person or some event. Performing in front of a crowd is one such event. The drug is adrenaline. Adrenaline is produced naturally by our bodies when we are in danger of being hurt in some way.

The problem with the adrenaline high is that it is so intense and overwhelming that the power it gives you can be addictive and it takes a long time to come down. Adrenaline is probably the number one problem in the law enforcement community. Cops are continually dealing with the problem of winding down after a shift, especially in ghettos and high crime areas where they are often in danger. The high levels of adrenaline they produce cause sleepless nights, and the constant lack of sleep leads to anger-management problems, which in turn can lead to relationship problems and alcohol abuse.

The best antidote for excess adrenaline, in my humble but experienced opinion, is pot! Marijuana, hemp, weed, da kind, whatever you want to call it. You see, pot actually counters the effects of adrenaline because it slows you down. Pot sits you down, mellows you out, and in some cases, puts you to sleep. And it does this without the bad side effects of alcohol. Alcohol will also slow you down, but its killing effects will eventually catch up with and destroy you, whereas pot has no known adverse side effects or the lingering problems of addiction. Apparently, you can become "mentally" addicted to it, but so far, no studies have shown that you can actually become physically addicted.

According to news reports, many professional athletes have been known to smoke pot recreationally. In fact, hardly a day goes by without news of some famous athlete being arrested for the possession of marijuana somewhere in America.

I was introduced to pot by a Chinese jazz musician in Calgary, Canada, in 1957. He gave me a joint and a Lenny Bruce record and changed my life forever. The joint lasted almost a month because I would take a hit, put it out, and then pull out the Lenny Bruce record and listen to comedy that had me falling on the floor laughing so hard and loud that on many occasions, I scared my mother.

I became a "one-hitter" mainly because pot was so hard to find back in the fifties. This was the reefer madness period, when people thought that smoking that evil weed would make you murder your family with an ax. People were doing heavy jail time for pot, people like Robert Mitchum, who did a year in county jail for possession of one marijuana cigarette. And *I* felt bad when I did nine months for a bong! Yeah, the more things change, the more they stay the same.

Listening to Lenny under the influence of pot gave me a goal in life. I knew what I wanted to do. I wanted to experience life to the fullest. I wanted to hit the road and travel and see for myself what was out there. Lenny made me laugh, but he also made me think. He made me realize that there were problems—

real problems—with the way the police and judges treated minorities and poor people. Lenny made me realize how bogus the system really is, how hypocritical religion is—all organized religions that exclude the rest of the world because they are somehow the "true" faith. Pot made me realize how organized religion has screwed up the world with all the fighting and bickering over whose god is the real god.

Lenny also addressed the race issue in America. He was the first comic to make it disappear with humor. He showed me what a powerful force humor was. He made me feel proud of who I was. Lenny gave me direction and a cause to believe in. Years later, when Cheech and I recorded our comedy albums, I could feel Lenny's presence in the studio with us.

There would not have been a Cheech and Chong had there not been pot and Lenny Bruce. Just like there would not have been Motown, or the Beatles, or Bob Dylan, for that matter, because pot rules! Pot has played a big role in the evolution of the human species since the very beginning of the Stone Age. The ten-million-year-old dude they found frozen in a glacier was wearing hemp clothing and a Cheech and Chong T-shirt, proving that pot has been around for a very long time.

The Rolling Stones event was a benefit concert for Nicaraguan earthquake victims, hosted by Mick Jagger's then wife, Bianca Jagger, at the Forum, the home of the Los Angeles Lakers. It was 1973 and we had just recorded our first comedy album; opening for the Stones was Lou's way of launching it. "And now ladies and gentlemen, let's get the show on the road. Please welcome Ode Recording stars Cheech and Chong."

I thought, *Well, there it is, folks, our first big-time introduction and he pronounced our name correctly*, which was a first.

Before that night, all the jazz and blues clubs that Cheech and I had been performing at in L.A. always messed up our names when they introduced us. In fact, one emcee, Norma Miller at the Redd Foxx Club—the very first club we performed at in Los Angeles—called us "Geek and Gank." I remember thinking to myself, *No, Bitch! It's Cheech as in peach and Chong as in dong.* But the mispronunciations never really bothered us because we were comedians. We made a living being laughed at, and the crowd at the Forum laughed at every skit that night. We were a rare, unexpected treat, because we could entertain music people. We could do what no comic had been able to do before us and very few have done since. Because we were musicians we could do our act for people who were used to hearing loud rock music. We understood what made musicians laugh and we had the material and the rhythm needed to pull it off. And we were Chicano. Actually, I was and still am half Chinese and half Caucasian, but that night, I was Chicano.

Ours was the typical rags to riches story, with the twist that we never really got out of the rags. The scruffy look was a big part of our persona. Cheech and Chong. The Lowrider and the Hippie. Together we recorded and sold millions of albums, acted in and directed six major motion pictures, and appeared on almost every major television talk show during the seventies and part of the eighties.

This is our story.

I know some of you will thumb through the book and go directly to the end to find out what happens. Well, don't waste your time. Because that is not the way I write. I write, as Cheech used to say, "Chinese style," which means all over the place. So get comfortable, sit back, and enjoy the read.

THE UNAUTHORIZED
AUTOBIOGRAPHY

CHAPTER ONE

WHAT'S THE HASSLE, MAN?

Los Angeles, California, 2007

My wife and I were sitting in the United Airlines terminal at Los Angeles Airport when I saw him walking toward me. It was Cheech. He was engaged in conversation with a man whom I assumed was his driver, so he didn't see us sitting there. I nudged Shelby and she looked up from the magazine she was absorbed in to look at Cheech. We watched as he approached us, walking with a slight O. J. shuffle, indicating a pair of battle-scarred knees from years of skiing, basketball, and running around onstage doing a character called Alice Bowie.

Cheech looked a little older than he did the last time I saw him, which was back in July, when he and his manager, Ben, approached me with an offer to play our old show in Vegas. But he looked happy as he chatted with his driver. He passed within ten feet of where we were sitting, and I realized I did not have the urge to reach out and grab him, as I would have a few years before. In fact, I was amazed at the way I did not jump up and hug this man with whom I had been so close for more than twenty years. He was my partner, my brother, my closest friend, and together we changed the face of comedy in America and the rest of the world with our records, our movies, and our live shows. So why did I just watch as he passed by? Why didn't I call out to him to let him know I was there? That we were there. What caused the rift that has separated us for more than twenty years? Well, the only way to answer these questions is to go back to the beginning.

September 1967. The Vietnam War was boiling over. The North Vietnamese were fighting and losing people, but winning the war. America was in the midst of a culture clash between those who supported the war and those who opposed it. Student antiwar activists were rallying the pot-smoking hippies to protest and oppose the war any way they could. The establishment fought back by drafting anyone and everyone they could, especially those who opposed the war. They went after Chicanos and blacks and poor white hillbillies and filled the trenches and the graves with their bodies. The only escape was the North Country—Canada.

Cheech had burned his draft card in protest at an antiwar rally hosted by Muhammad Ali. Burning your draft card was the ultimate fuck-you gesture to the war-mongering American government, which was drafting young, healthy Americans to fight and die in its ill-conceived war. But once you burned your card, you had broken federal law and were open to prosecution. So Cheech had to leave the country of his birth a wanted man, a fugitive from justice. Cheech had arranged to go to Canada through a network of antiwar activists. He represented a turn in events for Mexican Americans. Instead of sneaking into the United States, he was sneaking out of it. He took a bus and entered Canada as a legal landed immigrant at the Montana-Alberta border, and then continued north to Calgary.

Cheech had been taking pottery classes in Los Angeles and had become quite addicted to it, so he found a world-class potter in Canada named Drahanchuk, who agreed to take him on as an apprentice. Drahanchuk lived in Bragg Creek, Alberta, a little town in the middle of an Indian reservation west of Calgary, just a little way from where I grew up. The Indian tribes in the area had migrated from the States about a hundred years earlier and settled on reservations all around Calgary. They, too, were escaping an unjust war and the U.S. Army.

Cheech had never been to Canada before, so he really wasn't ready for the harsh weather. When he arrived from California in September, he was dressed in a light summer jacket, a T-shirt, jeans, and sneakers. The day was balmy, but as night approached, the temperature dropped rapidly and the feeling of the first snowfall was in the still air. The cars roared by Cheech as he hitchhiked, shivering by the side of the road. He danced and shifted his weight from foot to foot, trying desperately to stay warm. And he wore the most pathetic expression on his face, trying to guilt drivers into stopping, but to no avail. Finally, a car rolled to a stop, but as the grateful Cheech reached for the passenger door, the driver rolled down the window and said, "You better cover your ears, you're going to freeze them off." And with that friendly bit of advice, she roared off into the fading, cold sunset.

Cheech's feet and ears were starting to feel numb, which meant he was starting to freeze to death. Just then, a late model pickup truck slowly pulled to a stop. This time the passenger side door opened and Cheech was invited into the warm cab. The sudden burst of warm air flowed over him as he sat shivering in the truck. The driver, a black man with the build and attitude of a professional boxer, greeted him with a chuckle. "How long you been out there, boy?"

Cheech tried to answer but he was still numb from the cold, so he muttered, "Too long!"

The man chuckled again, "You sure ain't from around here, are you? Where you from, anyway?"

"Los Angeles," Cheech said quietly.

"Los Angeles? Well, that explains how you're dressed. You best get some winter clothes because you isn't in Los Angeles now, boy. So where you headed?"

"I am going to Bragg Creek to work for a potter. Drahanchuk . . . you know him?"

"Yeah, I know that fool. He does make good pottery. Well, you're in luck cause that's where I'm going." The driver needed someone to keep him company and listen to his stories on the long drive to Bragg Creek—and he had stories. He was an American, a professional boxer who had discovered Canada during his fighting days, when he was a main-event lightweight contender fighting under the name of George Dunn.

He went on to tell Cheech that he owned a summer cabin in Bragg Creek and was on his way to winterize the place. George rambled on while Cheech tried to hide the pain he was feeling while his body slowly thawed out. The truck heater was blasting delicious, warm air, and within a few minutes Cheech dozed off and had a much-needed sleep. His mind wandered back to Los Angeles and to his home, where his mother and sisters lived. They had no idea Cheech was in Canada and they wouldn't find out about it until a few months later, when he wrote them to tell them that he was alive and well. Although he had broken the law, he was not technically a criminal—at least, not in the eyes of the Canadian government. In fact, they had granted him and others asylum from the Vietnam War. And most of the thousands of American youths who had fled the country to live in Canada rather than die in Vietnam were black and Chicano.

Cheech's dad, Oscar, would be affected the most by his son's defection. Oscar was a decorated war hero who served his country in the military and was still serving his country as a Los Angeles police officer. Oscar was a tough, hard-nosed cop, who occasionally slept with a loaded .45 under his pillow. It was a habit he picked up during his stint in the Marines and it scared his whole family. When Oscar had to be woken for work, the family flipped a coin to see who would get the job because he would sometimes wake up and point the loaded gun at the person disturbing his sleep.

Oscar was also tough in other ways. To supplement his police income, he would take on construction jobs, such as pouring cement patios, and of course, Cheech, being the only son, would be his assistant. The assistant was the guy who carried the bags of cement mix and did the mixing. Not the best job for a slightly built bookworm like Cheech. However, Oscar was determined to make a man of his gentle son, so he piled on the work. Cheech, on the other hand, was determined not to be turned into a slave, so they had their issues.

Being a cop, Oscar was also in daily contact with the Chicano gangs, who had a special dress code. These clothes were forbidden in the Marin household. Cheech, of course, was not gang material in any sense, since he was intelligent and got very good grades in school. He had a photographic memory and he devoured books. He was not going to become a dropout gang member, but Oscar had to be sure, so he pushed his son every chance he got—and he got plenty of chances. Cheech was constantly on probation with Oscar for failing to do various chores around the house. Cheech's mother, Elsie, was an angel who saved her son many times by covering for him, but he still clashed with Oscar, as teenage sons have clashed with their fathers since the beginning of time.

One time, Cheech had talked back to his father while being chewed out for skipping a chore. Oscar went after him and he took off running. Now, Oscar was in very good shape and had the stamina of a boxer, which he once was. Oscar could run, and he expected to catch his frail little son; however, it wasn't as easy as Oscar expected. In fact, the chase became a marathon, with Cheech staying just out of his reach. Oscar chased Cheech down the street, through back alleys, up stairs to another street, down that street to a park, through the park, down more alleys, and down more streets, until he finally gave up because he had to go to work. Cheech hovered outside the house that night until Oscar left for work and his mother came out to tell him the coast was clear.

The truck rumbled to a stop, waking Cheech out of a sound sleep.

"Well, we're here. This is where I turn off," the driver said. Cheech rubbed the sleep out of his eyes and looked around. It was snowing and he had no idea where he was. Big, fluffy snowflakes were falling gently to the newly covered ground. With the snow-covered fir trees the scene looked like a Christmas card. It was beautiful and cold. Cheech climbed out of the truck and watched as it rolled away into the night. The cold air felt refreshing to him as he walked toward a neon-lit café, which seemed to be the only sign of life in the little town. The quiet of falling snowflakes amplified the sound of his shoes as he crunched his way toward the café. This was a sound he would get used to, but right now it was new to him. The whole experience was new to him, and he felt joy and excitement welling up inside him as he opened the café door.

Inside, the mood was festive and bright. A jazz trio played soft, muted dinner music while a lone waitress chatted with a couple of locals who hung out at the place for lack of anywhere else to go. This was the only game in town, and the reason the empty café could afford a band was because the bandleader owned the establishment. He was Gordie Shultz, sax player-bandleader-café owner. Gordie had grown up in Calgary, and had played in the high school band as well as in the Canadian Army band. Cheech fit right in with the little jazz trio because their musical tastes were so alike. Cheech had emulated Johnny Mathis for years and even bore a slight resemblance to the famous crooner; when he sang "Misty" and "Chances Are," he won over every regular customer in the little café.

Cheech also scored a little cabin on the creek, which he rented from Mr. Dunn, the black boxer who had given him a ride on his first day as a landed immigrant. Cheech's little summer cabin was heated by a wood stove, which meant he had to find firewood almost daily. The cabin also came with an outhouse. Oh, yes, Cheech was paying some heavy dues for leaving America in a time of war.

Still, he loved the quietness of the snow-covered firs and cedars that grew in abundance in the area. He loved the mute poetry of the silence that filled the still, cold air at night, when every star in the sky was so bright that the light almost blinded him when he stared upward. Now properly clothed, Cheech could enjoy the crunch of the snow under his feet as he walked to and from the little jazz café. As an American in a sea of Canadian locals, he also became a minor celebrity.

Most Canadians hated everything about the war. Calgary was filled with antiwar protesters and peaceniks who would rather meditate than fight. The hippie population in Canada swelled to overflowing during the sixties and early seventies. Long hair, beaded buckskin jackets, and bell-bottom jeans were the uniform of the pot-smoking, hip generation, inspiring musicians and singers to follow suit or be branded "pigs." Cheech resisted the longhaired craze as long as he could. He kept his neat Johnny Mathis appearance right up until he met his soon-to-be partner—me, Tommy Chong.

In the meantime, Cheech had grown tired of being a donkey for the world-renowned potter in Bragg Creek, so when summer came he made his way to Banff to sample the latest in ski bunnies. Cheech was attracted to big money and the ski world was the winter home for big money—trust-fund babes galore, searching for good-looking ski bums with insatiable sexual appetites. Cheech fit right in with the ski bum crowd and soon he was mingling with the hot babes on the slopes.

The one minor problem Cheech had was that he did not know how to ski, a problem he soon tackled right after he secured a job as a short-order cook. Of course, when asked if he had any experience in the kitchen, Cheech gave the usual, "Of course, no problem, tons of experience, blah blah blah." Cheech always told people exactly what they wanted to hear because he knew he was talented enough to learn on the job.

He did know how to cook Mexican food, but was a little lacking when it came to Canadian cuisine. So when the order came in for a Denver sandwidge, he asked the head chef what kind of Denver sandwidge he should make. The cook, always too busy to even talk to underlings, muttered something about ham, so Cheech made the customer a ham sandwidge . . . which came flying back to the kitchen with specific instructions to make a gaddamn Denver sandwidge and quit fucking around.

The shortest distance between a sucker and his money is to say whatever's necessary to get the dough. The hustle was a natural way of life for Cheech. When a free concert was announced, Cheech and his buddies went to the parking area and charged five bucks a car for free parking. No one even questioned them. Canadians are so used to paying out money that all you had to do was ask.

His perfect life changed abruptly when he suffered a compound fracture to his left leg while skiing Cheech-style. This was the style of pointing the skis downhill and just going for it. He had plenty of warnings, like the time he skied across a parking lot and into the side of a bus, much to the amusement of the bus riders, because he did not know how to stop. It was *POW!* right into the bus, like in a Road Runner cartoon.

The broken leg was quite sickening, the bone protruding through the skin like a jagged piece of a bloody stick. The hospital hooked him up with a gorgeous blonde nurse from Australia who immediately fell for the bloke with the fucked-up leg. Cheech and Jan had a thing right up until Cheech was well enough to leave the hospital and come to Vancouver to seek his fortune. Somewhere in his travels, Cheech got into the Transcendental Meditation teachings of the Beatles' guru, Maharishi Mahesh Yogi, and became a serious devotee. Learning the art of meditation served him well over the next twenty years, because practicing meditation unlocked his talents, his dreams, and his curiosity for new experiences. When Cheech closed his eyes in meditation for the first time, he experienced an awakening that thrilled his soul. He found a world where he was the ruler and the ruled. He was master and servant. He became his own universe. And he could do it anywhere.

Vancouver proved to be the paradise Cheech had been seeking. To him, it was the most perfect place on the planet: Mountains and oceans blended together in harmony, like yin and yang; there was an abundance of oysters and clams on the rocky beaches; daylight would last for up to fifteen hours during summer; leaves would change color in a breathless display during the fall; moss and mushrooms covered hundreds of square miles of rain forest in some places; and giant cedar trees provided food and shelter for the thousands of native people who lived in peace for centuries in God's private gardens, waiting for eternity to continue.

And it was in Vancouver at a nightclub called the Shanghai Junk, located in the heart of Chinatown, where the historic meeting of Cheech and Chong took place.

CHAPTER TWO

DOES YOUR MAMA KNOW ABOUT ME?

Detroit, Michigan, 1967

While Cheech was in Canada avoiding the draft, I was in Detroit signing up for it. I had to if I wanted to obtain a green card, which would enable me to work in the States legally. I was never in favor of the Vietnam War, but I had four years of experience as a Canadian Army cadet so I knew the soldier's way, and if drafted, I would have served in the U.S. military. I think my pro-military attitude actually kept me out of the war. They rejected me on the grounds that I was married with two children and I had extremely flat feet. Also, they probably assumed I was some nutcase who really wanted to go.

I would have gone just to get that elusive green card. They are very hard to obtain, and unless you know someone, your application could take many years and cost many dollars. The someone I knew was Berry Gordy, the songwriting genius who was the founder and owner of Motown Records, the most successful black-owned business in the country.

Berry and Diana Ross had discovered my R & B band in Vancouver, B.C., at my brother's after-hours nightclub, where we played six nights a week. The club was called the Elegant Parlour and it was *the* place to go after hours in Vancouver during the sixties and seventies. The band didn't have a name when Diana Ross and the Supremes saw us, but we did have a sound. We had one of the best, unheralded singers in R & B history. His name was Bobby Taylor and he could sing like no other singer in his time. Bobby's range was legendary, and the tone and power of his voice could intimidate even the legends of Motown, who would all be in attendance whenever we performed in the Detroit area. It was quite satisfying to look out and see David Ruffin of the Temptations sitting with Mary Wilson of the Supremes and all of the Four Tops sitting with Stevie Wonder and Berry Gordy. They were all there to hear our band from Canada—the Motown band with more white guys than black guys.

We actually had more black guys when Berry and the Supremes discovered us, but two couldn't get across the Canadian border because of prior criminal records, so we replaced them with three of the best musicians in Canada—the white guys, Eddie Patterson on guitar, Robbi King on organ and keyboards, and Duris Maxwell on drums. The players replaced Leroy Harrison on keyboards and Freddy Miller on drums, left Vancouver to visit Freddy's people in San Francisco, and were detained at the American-Canadian border when they tried to reenter Canada. When we received the news that the guys were turned away we knew they had to be replaced. The Motown contract we had all signed contained a "morality clause" that stated nondisclosure of a criminal record would make the contracts null and void—and then we would be fucked.

It was a decision that would come back to haunt me years later, but it was the right thing to do at the time. Besides, we had a bigger and better sound with Robbi, Eddie, and Duris. In fact, it was a fabulous, mind-blowing mix of cultures, humor, and harmony. We had a special sound that comes once in a lifetime, and then only if you are lucky.

Although we were signed by the great Berry Gordy himself, we had to make our way to Detroit on our own unless we wanted to sit around and wait for Motown to send for us. We were ready to go, so we gigged our way to Detroit, starting with Seattle, Jimi's hometown. The venue was packed to overflowing and what a thrill it was! The last time I had played in Seattle was in 1958, with the Shades. We played a dance hall–roller rink and were embarrassed by a much better band that played our theme song better than we did. Our theme song was "Honky Tonk," parts one and two, by Bill Doggett, the all-time best guitar-sax-organ hit song ever to hit the Top Twenty. And it was entirely instrumental: no vocals, just hardcore, jazz-filled R & B. The lyrics to the tune came later. "Honky Tonk" was the first R & B song I learned, when I was seventeen years old. I spent the better part of a year learning that song, with its jazz lead-off guitar solo, note for note—or what I thought was note for note. We played it every night for at least ten years. Every night. "Honky Tonk." The first bars of the tune had everyone running for the dance floor. It was so clean and funky and simple that it made me cry with happiness and despair. The guitar work was and still is the most classic, simple, pure, and tasty.

We played our version of "Honky Tonk" in Seattle in 1958 and then had to listen to a band with an organ, a guitar, and a sax play the tune note for every perfect fucking note! Exactly like the record! Every single, crying, blue-feeling note was even better than on the original recording. I remember our band being very quiet on the long ride back to Vancouver. The Shades had just gotten our asses kicked big time by a much better band. I had my hat handed to me by a real jazz guitar player. I eventually learned the tune note for note, but it was embarrassing at the time. But redemption finally came nearly ten years later, with the Vancouvers.

The Vancouvers were the best that the city of Vancouver had to offer. After Seattle, we ended up in Los Angeles where we talked to a Motown writer-producer named Hal Davis. Hal had an office in the tower at Sunset and Vine, and Bobby Taylor had set up a meeting with him so that we could listen to a few tunes that he thought we might be interested in recording. It was hot in Los Angeles and extremely hot in Hollywood, so none of us was moving very fast. In fact, we almost got hit a few times while jaywalking. The only guy who knew what he was doing that day was Hal. Hal was deformed. He had a gimpy leg and a weird hip or something. And here he is yelling, "Get across the street before you get run over. You are not in Canada now."

I immediately thought, *You gimpy-legged motherfucker. You sideways-limping, red-sweater-wearing, circle-walking ... who you telling how to walk? We walk in a straight line, motherfucker! See ... We don't be hobbling around the fucking block trying to walk fifteen feet ...* I never said it, but I thought it.

The tunes Hal played for us were OK, not great, but OK. I never really thought about what Bobby should be singing. I had other things on my mind. Like two families—three, counting my mom and dad, four counting Shelby's mom and dad, five counting Maxine's (my first wife's) mom and dad. Besides, Tom Baird and I had written a song that we would record and make the Vancouvers famous.

Los Angeles had a music scene, but it was all in the recording studios. The best of the best were working overtime recording for top producers and making tons of money. But we were a club band at the time and we needed a club to show off our talent. We found a little spot on Crenshaw called Maverick Flats that fit our needs and we booked a memorable night there. The club was known for a great soul group that performed there called the Seven Souls. We were an unknown entity at the time, so we were booked to open for them. The soul music scene in Los Angeles was very competitive for reasons other than music. The lead singer of a soul group had his pick of the ladies. And the better the singer, the foxier the ladies. The Seven Souls were all lead singers, so Maverick Flats had an abundance of foxes in the audience, which naturally attracted the guys, which in turn led to big smiles at the box office.

Word about Bobby Taylor had filtered into Los Angeles and the club was packed to overflowing that night. Acts like the Fifth Dimension and Chaka Khan were in attendance, waiting to hear Bobby Taylor and his white guys from Canada. Well, we did not let them down. Bobby sang, we played, and the people were amazed. The hot tune of the night was our rendition of "My Girl," the Temptations hit written by Smokey Robinson. We had no way of knowing that this song was also the Seven Souls' big finisher. The difference was that they did a vocal version and sort of faked the instrumental part of the song whereas we did the Temptations' version right down to the string and horn arrangements (thanks to Eddie Patterson and Robbi King, whose classical music training enabled us to kick some major ass that night). We also dipped into *The Curtis Mayfield Guitar Songbook* with "People Get Ready" and "I Wonder," little-known songs that were lovingly hand-picked by Bobby, who had a special talent for finding obscure but memorable tunes that had people asking, "Is that original?" It was this attention to detail that impressed Berry Gordy enough to sign us.

I met Chaka Khan on the street in New York recently and she reminded me of that night. Forty years later and she still remembered. It *was* a night to remember. The Seven Souls took the stage after us, but not before they had a big argument in the dressing room right before going on. We heard them as we cleared our instruments off the stage. I knew exactly what they were going through. They lacked a Bobby Taylor. Bobby had taught us our sound and we had worked at it. He played the drums and the piano, and he knew what the bass and guitar were supposed to sound like. He arranged the vocal parts and taught me to sing notes that I never knew existed. He also taught me how to speak into a microphone. That is an art in itself.

That night we left the Seven troubled Souls to contend with playing for a very satisfied audience.

Although Bobby could sing, play music, and teach like no other, he carried his street attitude with him like a loaded gun. Bobby was raised in a tough New York ghetto, where he learned his craft on the street corners where other performers, such as Frankie Lymon of the Teenagers, learned to sing. Bobby seldom talked about his early life in New York except to say he never wore shoes that fit him properly until he lived in Columbus, Ohio, with his mother. In New York, his father used to stop at the Salvation Army and pick up a batch of different size shoes and dump them on the kitchen table. The kids would then have to grab a pair that fit. Bobby was one of the youngest so he just had to take whatever size was left when the others had picked. Scarred by the experience, he bought expensive shoes by the dozens when he did come into Motown money. Bobby was a product of the black nightclub culture of the fifties and sixties, with its "pimp, bitch, whore" mentality. An attitude that would keep young black men like Bobby from achieving the stardom that should have been theirs.

Somehow, men with this attitude actually attracted beautiful women in droves, and I wanted to know why. I understood

how women would be attracted to someone who sang as beautifully as Bobby, but I saw the same women fall all over themselves trying to get to a brother who, although attractive, sang
quite poorly.

I had to learn how to be a black man, so I studied every
chance I got.

CHAPTER THREE

INTRODUCING THE CALGARY SHADES

Calgary, Alberta, Canada, 1956

My first partner, Tommie "Little Daddie" Melton, was an ex-football star, who was being groomed for the pros when he suffered a terrible knee injury. Just before I met him, I was playing rhythm guitar for a full-blood Native American from the Stony Indian Reservation. His name was Dick Bird and his thing at the time was doing Elvis impersonations during lunch at Western Canada High School in Calgary. Dick would get the gigs and then call me in to be his backup guitarist. It always amazed me when the girls in the audience would scream and try to touch him while he was in Elvis mode. In these girls' minds, Dick *was* Elvis when he was onstage—even by proxy, Elvis was the god of rock and roll.

Dick loved to perform, so he hustled gigs wherever he could. The Canadian Legion was a good place to work because they had money and they loved being entertained while they drank their inexpensive beer. So every other weekend, Dick and I would do a forty-five minute set and be paid as much as fifty bucks a show.

It was my brother Stan who introduced me to Tommie. I had seen him dance at Bowness Park, a huge recreation park a few miles outside of Calgary. Tommie and a group of his black friends were the stars of the dance floor because they could cut a rug and dance like . . . well, black folks! Keep in mind there were not a whole lot of black folks in Calgary in the fifties. Just a few football stars with names like "Sugarfoot" Anderson and Woody Strode. And Tommie "Little Daddie" Melton.

When Tommie heard that I played guitar, he immediately wanted to form a band. So I talked Dick into including Tommie and his partner Eddie in the Legion Hall gigs as a dancing act. We formed a band over the next few weeks and started playing dances. My brother, Stan, played bass; with Bernie Sneed on the keyboards; Pete Watts, a very good-looking mixed-race dude, on the sax; Eric Murrey, a friend of Pete's, on the drums; me on the guitar; and Tommie and Dick sharing the singing duties. Dick, Eric, and Pete eventually split and formed their own band, leaving Tommie, Bernie, Stan, and me looking for a drummer. We eventually settled on Sunny Caruthers, a brother from Edmonton.

The black folks in Western Canada have quite a story themselves. I want to do a book about them one day because their story needs to be told. My life changed drastically when I was introduced to black culture. Everything about it was different. The music was unlike anything that played on the radio in Calgary, where one station, which played country music, ruled the airwaves for decades. This was the only music I had heard until I met Tommie and the rest of the brothers and sisters. Calgary in the fifties and sixties was more like Mississippi than California in the way that black people were treated. There were some diehard bigots in that city. We had a neighbor who named his black Labrador "Nigger." This guy would call his dog in at night by yelling "Nigger, here! Nigger, come on, boy." And nobody in the neighborhood thought anything of it.

There was one black girl in my whole high school, and she had to constantly bear the teacher's racist remarks. People were ignorant. They did not know any better. I remember attending a dance held in the East End and hearing a white guy ask a black dude, "Hey, Darkie, can you tell me what time it is?"

The black guy did not hesitate a second. *Bam!* One punch and Whitey was laid out cold. He probably wasn't unconscious, but he knew enough not to move after the punch. The dumb white guy didn't know any better; this was probably the first black guy he had ever talked to. Canadian schools did not address the race problem because, as far as they were concerned, there was no problem.

The Chinese in Canada were also treated poorly by the white ruling class. The Chinese were brought in as slave labor to build the railroad and were then told to get lost when it was finished. The blacks came to Canada to escape the hatred and dangers of the American South. They wagon-trained all the way to the area north of Edmonton, where they settled in the beautiful Amber Valley. And the Native Americans, or Indians, were there from even earlier, when some of the southern tribes were chased up to Canada by the U.S. Army.

So there we were—Tommie, a descendant of slaves; Dick Bird, a Native American from the Sarcee tribe; and me, of Chinese-Scottish-Irish descent. Together we represented the different shades of color, so we called ourselves The Shades. Although Tommie and Dick sang lead, I was the unofficial leader because I had more show business experience than the others. When I was ten years old, my fiddle-playing neighbor taught me two important things: the first was to keep it simple, and the second was that the audience rules. Always give the audience what they want. If they came to dance, then play dance music. If they came for a show, then give them a show.

The Shades were high-energy. We were playing at the very beginning of rock and roll, the fifties—Chuck Berry, Little Richard, Bo Diddley, and the King himself, Elvis. We quit doing Elvis when Dick left the band to go solo; Chuck Berry was our rock-and-roll model. We learned every Chuck Berry song ever written. I even have a deformed right thumb from playing Chuck Berry–style boogie guitar.

Chuck Berry had a sound all his own. He would play eighth notes on downstrokes on the fifth and sixth strings with a boogie rhythm while he sang, and he played in sax and piano keys, which were C, D, E-flat, and B-flat. He seldom played in guitar chords like E or A, where you had open strings to play with. No, it was the goddamn C and D, where you had to do bar chords and play boogie on the top strings all at a frantic tempo. The reason Chuck played these chords was because he always played with jazz piano players! The early black rock-and-roll artists were really great jazz musicians who just wanted a paycheck, so they played rock and roll with jazz techniques. Motown would come along later and really exploit these great jazz musicians, who played on hit records and were paid scale to help create the songs, while the songwriters and producers took the bulk of the cash.

Bo Diddley was another rock and roll hero of mine. I loved Bo's lyrics, as did the Rolling Stones and Buddy Holly. In addition to playing Chuck Berry and Bo Diddley songs, The Shades performed Little Richard, Sonny Boy Williamson, and Muddy Waters tunes to a blues-starved Calgary audience, who would get so riled up listening to us that they would practically riot in the streets after the dances.

Our band was so hot that the owners of Bowness Park hired us on reputation alone. But we were so new to the music business that when the local musician's union representative came by rehearsal to tell us we had to join the union, we thought the guy was a nutcase trying to extort money from the band. The guy who ran the dance hall finally paid our dues and we were an instant success.

We had that gig for the entire summer. Eventually, I put a group of singers behind Tommie that made us sound more like another one of our heroes, Fats Domino. A singer from New Orleans, Fats was riding high with his hits, "Blueberry Hill," "Blue Monday," and "Walking to New Orleans." We covered his songs and had the dancers in Calgary following us to every gig within two hundred miles. And when Tommie sang "What Am I Living For?" by Chuck Willis, girls would always cry at the beauty of the lyrics.

We were the hot band in Alberta. Rock and roll was a religion back in those days and we were its high priests. We toured the region, playing wherever we could find a venue, and a loyal group of fans followed us everywhere. The interior of Alberta is the heart of Canada's wheat-growing bread basket, which meant we played to a lot of farm folks. Most members of the younger generation who attended our dances were very cool and respectful, but now and then a drunken idiot would show his ignorance and the fight would be on. We were so compelling onstage, however, and our show would put everyone in such a good mood, that we would get through the night with maybe just a fight or two at the end.

One time we were in a resort area called Sylvan Lake for a gig at a dance hall. During the day we found a horse rental stable and rented most of their horses. The locals, upon seeing black men on horses, freaked out and called the local cop, who immediately rounded up all the black people he could find and held them until he was satisfied that we were indeed a group of musicians and not a band of escaped chain-gang convicts. The redneck cop had to let us go because we had not broken any laws. In fact, the rental stable had been more than glad to get our business. This incident made me aware of the extreme ignorance that existed in the country of our birth. If you white, you all right, if you brown, you can stick around, but if you black, get back!

The Shades had a fabulous run in Calgary in the late fifties, but all good things must come to an end. And in the end, our success and popularity drove us out of town.

One day we were summoned to the mayor's office, where we were met by the chief of police, the mayor, and a representative from the Canadian Legion Hall, where we performed every Saturday night. The mayor of Calgary at the time was an ex-DJ by the name of Don McKay, who was famous for giving white cowboy hats to visiting celebrities and dignitaries. We ran a teen dance club and the money we collected went into a teen fund—after the band was paid, of course. When I look back now, I see very clearly that I had a social conscience. Because we had formed the teen club, the city could not just shut us down. No, they had to ask us to leave town in a quiet, polite manner, which they did over the objections of the Legion Hall official, who loved renting out the hall to us.

Leave town? Did I just hear the mayor of Calgary ask us very nicely to "leave town"? This was something out of a Wild West movie! "Say, partner, y'all best be leaving town now. Don't want to have to put you in jail, so you boys best take your black rock-and-roll asses out of Calgary!"

We looked at one another and smiled at the prospect of going on the road. Our drummer-manager at the time, Sunny Caruthers, called some connections in Vancouver and got us work in the most beautiful city in the world. This was in the winter of 1958, probably one of the coldest winters on record.

I can say that without research because every winter in Calgary during the fifties was the coldest fucking winter on record. My father was born in Vancouver and every once in a while he would talk about the fruit trees, the ocean, and what it was like growing up there. I had an image of the place in my mind and I was ready to move there. I was a twenty-year-old blues musician and had lived in one cold-ass place all my life, so I was more than ready for a new location.

We arrived in Vancouver during one of the worst snowstorms in the city's history. Driving was all but impossible. But Sunny's old Buick just cut through the snow like a plow and took us right to our first gig. The club was a supper club that featured family-style entertainment in the form of a doorman who would sing songs from *Oklahoma!* It was located on the second floor of the hotel where we were staying, which made it easy to show up on time. But when the club manager saw that we were a band of color, he immediately made it clear that his club was owned and operated by the IMF—the Ignorant Motherfuckers union of fat gangster wannabes. We were told to eat in the kitchen and not to associate with the waitresses. Our first reaction to their orders was, "Where are the waitresses?"

The club owners did not know who they were dealing with—we were, in essence, a punk band that played rhythm and blues. You tell us we are not welcome as equals and you will suffer the consequences. Our band was made up of some tough Canadian fuckers who enjoyed fighting against assholes! We had Tommie Melton, the semipro football player who had fought in the ring as a pro boxer, and Bernie Sneed, who played football, hockey, and spent quite some time in the gym working on his perfect build. Bernie was a tough street fighter—so tough that he would fight for fun. But our toughest fighter was probably my brother, Stan, who had played semipro football and industrial league hockey. Fortunately, he stayed home with his wife and baby girls or else he would have been butting heads with the club owners.

The club was so wrong for our band it was pathetic. But from the moment Tommie grabbed the mic and went into the first song, the mood changed instantly from soft to hard, from fluff to substance—in a drumbeat! We rocked the club so hard that night, the customers never knew what hit them. And to top off the evening, we added a jazz trio, with our sax player Ken Chaney playing incredible jazz piano, me on bass, and Sunny on drums. We were such a hit that we disregarded all of the *Sopranos*-wannabe owners' rules about eating in the kitchen and not fraternizing with the customers or waitresses, as one table after another invited us to sit and drink with them. (Sunny ended up marrying one of the waitresses we were supposed to stay away from, and Tommie Melton went with the other one for a year.) The next day the club owner fired us. No reasons were given. Sunny then secured us a gig at a club down the street, where again we thrilled the audience but pissed off the manager.

Right after we were fired from *that* club, Sunny left immediately to secure us another job, leaving Ken with the car keys and instructions on where to meet him. Our routine after every gig was to find a Chinese restaurant and chow down. So there we were—everyone except Sunny—eating and chatting with the waitresses whom we had been ordered to stay away from. About three quarters of the way through the meal, we noticed three taxicabs pull up in front of the café and park. We also noticed about eight big men exit the cabs, each carrying a baseball bat. One of the waitresses exclaimed, "I don't believe this. Hey, Marlene, look what the cat dragged in," as the big—and I mean very big—thugs entered the restaurant. Each of them took up a position behind one of the guys at the table, while the leader told the girls, "Get your asses up and get in the cabs." The girls just sat there. I guess they were waiting for the band to do something. It was a good thing they finally got up and did what they were told, because otherwise we would still be sitting there now. The girls left and the big hulks followed them out the door, where they all got into the cabs and drove off.

We just sat there looking at one another. It really was a frightening feeling sitting there helpless with a big guy standing over you, a baseball bat in his hands and a real mean look on his face. Someone broke the ice by saying, "That was some scary shit that just happened!"

"Who the fuck were those guys? Man! I don't believe this!"

"Well, believe it because it just happened! Hey, man, look! The girls are running back." We all looked out the window and, sure enough, the girls were running and laughing like maniacs!

"We jumped out at the light. Fuck those guys! They ain't my father!" The girls were laughing about as hard as we were not laughing. We all looked at one another, and all thinking the same unspoken thought, we all scrambled to get the fuck out of there! We all piled into the Buick and drove off, passing a cab from the same cab company that had just brought our worst nightmares to the café. When the cab suddenly made a U-turn and came after us, we knew we were in trouble—big trouble, because the Buick was on its last legs and could not go more than twenty miles an hour.

The cab pulled up behind us and started blowing its horn. Ken jammed his foot on the gas pedal, forcing an extra mile an hour out of the tired car. Bernie and I were frantically looking for a weapon of some kind. We needed something, anything! Then our car came to a slow, sputtering stop as the motor died.

We all jumped out and realized we were in some kind of dead-end alley. There was no escape!

We turned and faced the cab, unable to see anything because of the headlights glaring at us. I think we were all about to fall on our knees and beg for mercy when a familiar voice came from behind the lights.

"What is wrong with you guys? Didn't you hear us honking?"

"Sunny? Is that you?"

"Yeah, it's me, and what did you do to my car?"

"Man, we thought you were the guys from the club."

"Hey, we got us a gig at the New Delhi starting tomorrow." After Sunny told us the good news, we told him about the goons at the club who had threatened us.

"Fuck those motherfuckers! They better not come around the Delhi with that 'eat in the kitchen' shit! There be some bad-ass brothers at this club who will take those baseball bats and make the motherfuckers eat them!"

Sunny was a tough little guy. He and the waitress he married eventually split, but not before they had a couple of kids. Sunny had been a uranium miner in the fifties, before they found out how bad it was for you, and he was diagnosed with some strange form of cancer and died about ten years after we hooked up with him.

We found a home at the New Delhi, a rhythm-and-blues club located on the corner of Keefer and Main. This was a real down-home blues club, complete with a jukebox and a house band. We were the floor show and the crowds loved us so much that we were held over for a year!

Even though we stayed in Vancouver, that year at the New Delhi taught me all I needed to know about the road.

CHAPTER FOUR

GET BACK TO WHERE YOU ONCE BELONGED

Calgary, Alberta, Canada, 1960

The Shades fell apart when the gig at the New Delhi finally came to an end. We played at the New Delhi for as long as we could, and then Bernie and I made our way back to Calgary, where I worked as a truck driver for a year. We tried forming a band, but we missed the spark and excitement that we had with Tommie Melton. Bernie and I stayed in Calgary and tried to go straight—that is, to hold down a job—but the memories of Vancouver were too strong. Once you get a taste of being in the spotlight and having people clap and cheer for you, nothing else can replace that feeling.

I was dating Bernie's sister, Maxine, at the time. I came back to Calgary to be with her, but ultimately she dumped me because I had become just another uneducated laborer who drove a truck for Canadian Freightways. When I was a musician in a hot band I was attractive and sexy, but as a truck driver I was grimy and not so sexy. So Maxine started seeing other guys and I went on the hunt for other black girls.

I eventually met a tall, beautiful seventeen-year-old named Gail, who was extremely intelligent and had a wicked sense of humor. And although I had seen her in person only a couple of times, we started a torrid phone affair, talking every night for hours. I was in love with her voice and her personality, so naturally I asked her to marry me. I was still in love with Maxine, but Maxine was cruising along fine without me. I was lonely and I wanted a family of my own. I felt like an old man at the ripe age of twenty, and I desperately wanted to grow up and have kids like all the other truck drivers I was working with.

I bought Gail a ring and proposed to her. She laughed and accepted the proposal and we made love to seal the deal. I loved her over the phone, but things were different in person, and I had this little nagging feeling that this wasn't right. I didn't feel the same way about her that I felt about Maxine. That special spark was missing. Later that week I realized I did not love Gail. The twin Gemini personalities in me had a talk, and both decided I was too young to be married. So I called it off. Gail was very cool about it. She even returned the ring. But there was something different about the way she looked. There was a glow about her that I hadn't seen before and a beauty that made me wonder if I was doing the right thing. But then I realized that I could not live a straight life. The taste of the Vancouver nightlife was still with me and I wanted to go back. Living in Calgary without a band was too fucking boring. Bernie was feeling the same way, so when Tommie called and told us about a new club that wanted the Calgary Shades, it only took us a minute to decide.

I owned a '53 Chevy at the time and I was ready to rumble off to Vancouver—and rumble we did. We drove over the mountains again, for the second time in three years, only this time it was just the two of us. The trip was uneventful . . . until we reached the top of the mountain range, and disaster struck. The plate connecting the front wheel to the frame broke in two. The car would not steer. Fuck! Right in the middle of the mountains. There was only one thing to do and that was to fix it ourselves.

It is impossible to find parts for used cars in the middle of the mountains, and even if we could, we could not afford them, so I crawled under the car and assessed the damage. I am about as far away from a natural mechanic that one can be and still love cars, so crawling under and looking at the damage was pure instinct I inherited from my father, who drove trucks for a living and always had oil-stained hands. The bracket that attached the wheel had split right in the middle, forcing the left front wheel to lean against the frame, which made driving impossible. We were in the middle of nowhere, but somehow we were lucky enough to break down right next to a service station. The kid at the station just pumped gas, so I asked if I could borrow some tools and he sort of shrugged and said, "They don't belong to me, 'cause I just pump gas."

I grew up in Canada so I know how to talk to Canadians, especially mountain boys who are basically socially retarded. It's not that they don't want to help; they do. But they know their limitations. They have been told all their lives how stupid they are and, like most people, they believe everything they are told. Living in a huge country populated by folks who have never been in a crowd does strange things to people, especially when confronted by problems that require the formation of an opinion.

Some Canadians have been alone so long that the sound of their own voices tends to frighten them. There is a condition that affects people who are alone in the mountains for too long. It's called being bushed. People who are away from other human beings for too long tend to create their own reality, which, in reality, is unreality. When confronted with that type of person you have to take action. And you don't ask questions or ask for opinions. I just acted like the garage belonged to me and found all the tools needed to repair the broken strut. Then I drilled a couple of holes and bolted a solid piece of metal across the break and it was good to go. I returned the tools to their proper drawers, thanked the kid, and we drove off.

We made it to Vancouver without any further mishaps, thanks to the grace of God, and Bernie and I were back in the band and back in the music business. Vancouver nightlife embraced us like old friends, and soon we were back with the pimps, whores, and hustlers, feeling right at home again. Bernie and I agreed that the straight life was not for us. We needed the nightlife like a vampire needs blood. The reunion gig was at a club called The Moon Glow Cabaret. The Moon Glow was owned by Daddy Clark, a railway porter who loved The Shades and wanted to see us back together. Railway porters played a big part in our development as blues musicians because they were the ones who brought records up from the States, turning us on to Hank Ballard and the Midnighters, who did tunes like "Sexy Ways," "Annie Had a Baby," and "The Twist." They brought us the latest records from Bo Diddley, Muddy Waters, and a host of other blues artists who were otherwise unobtainable. We would learn these great tunes and then play them for a grateful audience, who would be hearing them for the first time, since they were never played on the radio.

I moved back into the Hazelwood Hotel, where I had been living the year before, and was greeted like a long lost son by the Chinese owners, who had met my parents when my folks drove out to pick me up the previous year. The hotel was really a whorehouse, so I was a little uneasy about having my parents stay there. But being Chinese, my pop would have it no other way. Pop and the owners had a great time talking in Chinese about the old days. They even put my mom and pop up in a suite that I never knew existed. I was always in a single room with a bath on the fourth floor, facing Hastings Street. The rooms were always warm and clean and cheap and within walking distance to all the East End clubs.

There was a young prostitute at the Hazelwood who used to hide in my room from her pimp, who would beat her daily. It was kinda weird at first, but eventually I got used to the ways of the street. And pimp beatings were the order of the day with those folks. The young girls, who were usually strung out on junk, gave all their money to these pimps, who were more like dog trainers. They had to discipline the girls constantly to keep them prostituting themselves. It was a very sick society. I would have made a lousy pimp. I would try on occasion to talk the girls out of "working," and I refused to take money from them. I did not have the "pimp" mentality. The club paid enough to pay rent but toward the end of the week money would be very hard to come by, so I had a system where I would purchase meal tickets from the little café across the street, but the food was so bad that I ended up living on the one meal a night that we got from the club, which was a bowl of curry chicken and a couple of roti (Indian bread).

But Chinatown was just a block away, and if you knew your way around Chinatown, you could eat on the cheap. Good wholesome food, too. The Chinese have always found ways to feed the hungry. We found a place called the Green Door where you could eat a meal for two dollars! Beef and vegetables over a bowl of rice for two bucks!

The year was 1961 and Vancouver's weather was dull and dreary. We barely saw daylight anyway because we usually slept all day and played all night. Christmas was a very Spartan affair that year, but it became a little homier when I received a care package from my mother. It was a simple cardboard box filled with Christmas goodies that I shared with my fellow musicians. I received another present later that year when Gail informed me that she had given birth to a beautiful eight-pound baby girl, whom she named Rae Dawn. My mother was very happy because Gail, who was only seventeen years old at the time, brought Rae Dawn to my parents so they could look after her while she finished school.

Later that year I received a call from Maxine, who was ready to get married. I was more than thrilled—I still loved Maxine and I wanted to marry her, even though I was having a great time being single in Vancouver. By then the Moon Glow had closed down and we were all playing different gigs with different bands. Bernie was playing piano at the Harlem Nocturne on Hastings, while I was playing on weekends with La Vern Gerard, a tall mixed-race singer from Vancouver. I was also playing guitar at various illegal booze clubs downtown. These clubs had sprung up all over the city during the fifties, when Vancouver's blue laws forced legally licensed clubs to close at midnight on Saturday, and prevented liquor from being served anywhere on Sunday! It was the Canadian version of Prohibition. The government controlled the liquor industry; in fact, you could only buy booze from the Liquor Control Board. But beer sold for ten cents a glass or $2.50 for a dozen bottles, and minimum wage was $1.25 an hour.

The club where Cheech and I met had a history in Vancouver dating back to the blue laws days, when all the East End clubs operated without liquor licenses, catering to the low life and the high life of Vancouver club goers. Originally called the Kubla Klan, the name was changed to the Shanghai Junk by the family who renovated the place and obtained a liquor license. The old Kubla Klan held about three hundred people comfortably and up to five hundred, uncomfortably, on the weekends.

The BYOB club goers were of the hard-nosed working class, with a few professionals from the nicer regions of Vancouver thrown in on the weekends. Since the club was across the street from the police station and during the fifties, the police were on the take, the Kubla Klan survived. However, the liquor license did not go over well with the bring-your-own-bottle club goers, so they eventually stopped showing up, and within a few years the Junk was losing money.

Bernie and I flew back to Calgary for my wedding, which took place on September 23, 1961, Maxine's birthday. It was an exciting time for me because I was seeing and holding my daughter for the first time. Rae Dawn was almost seven months old the first time I held her. She had a killer smile and her eyes twinkled as I held her. I pressed my face against her head and took in the clean, delicious baby smell, while her little brown hands tried to take off my glasses. The feeling of holding your very own baby for the first time is magical and filled with spirit. And that feeling of love is so overwhelming that tears of joy flow naturally, as if to relieve the pressure of so much happiness. This little bundle of love who smiles and coos baby sounds at you is a part of you. And it humbles you, for you are in the presence of Love made Flesh. Rae Dawn attended the wedding with her grandmother (my mom), who held her tight in her skinny little arms. My mother would later be awarded custody of my first little daughter.

When we arrived back in Vancouver, Maxine immediately found a job as a secretary for a large firm located on Powell Street and Granville. I went down to the unemployment office and found employment of sorts as a salesman for a bakery. It was a small, family-owned bakery that specialized in fresh baked bread and an assortment of sweets. My job was to drive around the neighborhood giving away free bread to lure in new customers. I tried that for about a month but failed to attract any new customers, so I had to find another form of employment.

I had connected with an agency called the Hooper Holmes Corporation that specialized in investigating people who bought insurance—car insurance, life insurance, and so on. This firm investigated would-be customers for various insurance companies to make sure they were who they claimed to be. I knew the district manager, who was an ex-cop from Calgary, so I was hired almost immediately.

I had been a greasy, dirty-fingernails, grubby-clothes type of worker who longed to be able to wear a suit and tie and be clean when I got home from work. So I was delighted when I finally landed the job I coveted, and in no time I was an investigator. The day of my first client investigation, I knocked on a neighbor's door to inquire whether the "client did in fact reside at that address." The lady stared at me for a long time before asking, "Well, who are you and why do you want to know?" The sudden question flustered me, as I stammered, muttered something, and handed her my business card. She looked at the card and then slammed the door in my face. I stood there for a moment before making my way back to my car, where I sat contemplating my approach. It was too direct. Too coplike. People automatically stiffen up when they have to talk to cops. I had to change my tactics. On the next client, I tried a different approach.

"Hey, how are you doing? Listen, I am looking for a place to rent in the neighborhood, and I was wondering if you could help me. I just arrived in town and I love this area." This approach would put people at ease, especially when I told them how much I loved their neighborhood. And they would start commenting on the neighbors. They would tell me if they were decent, and sometimes they would rat them out—either way, I would get an idea of who they were, how many people lived in the house, and who owned and drove the car.

I loved the job because I was unsupervised and I could come and go as I pleased as long as I did my quota of investigations. It was undercover police work, and I got a thrill whenever I uncovered something. The one skill that remains with me today is my ability to size people up by observing them. You can tell a lot about people from the touch of their hands and how they walk. This skill came in handy when Cheech and I started recording our comedy albums and filming our movies, because we could get inside the many characters that we introduced to the stoner public.

Maxine got pregnant soon after we were married and gave birth on May 28, 1963, to the most beautiful little baby girl in the world since Rae Dawn was born. Black curly hair, big brown eyes, and skin the color of mocha. She looked so delicious, people just wanted to pick her up and eat her. Rae Dawn now had a little sister, Robbi, and the two of them were so beautiful that they would stop traffic wherever they went.

One time they got into a bottle of aspirin and freaked everyone out. We could not determine whether they ate the aspirin, so we rushed them to the emergency room. The staff at the hospital loved them so much, they kept them overnight for observation, even though they were running around with no side effects from having taken any medication. The nurses had the two little brown beauties on display, and patients and staff from all areas of the hospital dropped by just to look at them. My beautiful girls both went on to enjoy successful movie and television careers. Who would have thought, eh?

Back then I was still playing guitar on the side for Tommie. We both loved music so much that money was never our reason for performing. Tommie would find gigs for us at local community halls and school dances, and he would also scour the neighborhood for halls to rent where we could throw our own dances. Eventually he came across a converted movie theater with a For Rent sign. The Alma Theatre was located in Vancouver's West End, on Ninth and Alma. The owner had the slanted floors leveled for dancing, but he kept the balcony and the rest of the movie décor. When Tommie showed me the place, I fell in love with the whole building. We arranged to pay three hundred dollars a month in rent; the only problem was that neither Tommie nor I had any money.

Having the theater proved a challenge. We named it the Blues Palace and set about figuring out how to attract people to the place. Our band was not a big enough draw, since people could see us playing all over the city. Our only hope was to book a name. We drove down to Seattle one weekend and hooked up with a local promoter in the black part of town. We found him by copying his name and number off one of the posters that was on a telephone pole in the middle of the 'hood. He was very glad to meet us when we told him we wanted to book his acts in our club in Vancouver. He showed us his roster of acts and when we saw Ike and Tina Turner we both said, "Uh, how much for them?"

As luck would have it, he had a Tuesday open for only seven hundred dollars. One night, two shows, including a ten-piece band, three backup singers, Ike, Tina, at least three roadies, and one manager. Our new band, Little Daddie and the Bachelors, played during intermission. I was thrilled when Ike and a couple of his musicians came and stood in front of my amp to listen to me play. Our drummer, Ted Lewis, commented that, "Ike came and listened to you, man." That night Ted heard the drums played like he had never heard before. Ike's drummer tore up the room, kicking ass with his gospel-style bass drum, drumming with tempos and beats never before heard in Canada.

The whole band had a groove that gave everyone in the place a high that lasted for two decades. Tina was a wonder—a pure African sex goddess with energy and edginess that complemented her husky voice. When Tina sang, the mic became a big, hard cock and it was your cock that she was breathing hot, sultry lyrics into, at times pressing her beautiful lips against the substitute penis. The Ikettes moved and danced with the precision of ancient, tribal, ritualistic mating dances—voodoo dolls moving in close formation, driving taut, hard dancer bodies with the hypnotic rhythms of ancient Africa. If Tina was the African goddess, then Ike was the tall, skinny African king. He commanded the stage like an emperor, leading the band with the chopping motions of his Fender Stratocaster, which he waved like a Samurai warrior, slashing the blues-packed air as he signaled the music breaks in each song. The Vancouver audience ate them up; the concert was an astounding success. Tommie and I made enough money to pay off our one investor, the rent, and the Ike and Tina revue, and the rest went into our pockets.

I went to work the following Monday with a pocketful of cash. I made more money that night than I would make all month at the Hooper Holmes Corporation, so I handed in my resignation. But as fate would have it, our success as booking agents was short-lived. In fact, Ike and Tina was the only act we ever booked. The problem was that we wanted to *be* Ike and Tina, playing the blues to screaming, adoring fans. That was our goal. The Blues Palace was only open for a couple of weeks before we were called before City Hall again. The neighborhood was up in arms about us having a blues club in their prissy, white little area and asked the city to shut us down. *Here we go again*, I thought. But I understood the neighbors' complaints. Our club attracted drunk teenagers who had no respect for anyone. They would piss wherever they felt like and drink beer wherever they felt like, leaving the nice, trimmed lawns covered with beer bottles and puke. So we closed the place down and went looking for another club.

We found an empty restaurant in Chinatown on Pender between Columbia and Main. It was quite small, but was located in an area where people urinated and puked on the sidewalks without generating complaints. Once again, Tommie and I had the task of building and opening a blues club, T's Cabaret, and we were in heaven. The band had been pared down to a quartet by then. Bernie Sneed took his B3 organ and began performing with his own group, leaving Tommie on vocals, Wes on bass, Duris on drums, and me on guitar. We packed the club every Friday and Saturday, but it was very slow during the week.

The truth is, neither Tommie nor I had any business sense. We were both high school dropouts and it showed. But we loved the life. We loved performing. We loved the blues. Tommie's magic was in his performances. The physical way he handled the mic would mesmerize the audience, especially the girls. Tommie's sexuality would attract women of all ages, married, single—they were all attracted to his physical beauty and the way he would make them each think, *this is all for you, baby*. Tommie was like many blues sex gods before him, men like Sonny Boy Williamson, Bo Diddley, and Muddy Waters. These men commanded sexual obedience from their fans. And they got it.

I, on the other hand, was the opposite of Tommie. In all ways. I was a little on the skinny side. I wore glasses and played backup guitar. And although I made most of the decisions for the band, I was never a leader in the usual sense of the word. I was the nerdy guy who had a thing for black girls. I loved black girls because I loved being a black man. I became black soon after I met Tommie. In fact, when Tommie lived at our house for a brief period, I took lessons from him. I tried his workout routine, which at one time included running five miles before breakfast. Uh, I did that once. It was brutal because it wasn't just running. It was running up hills and down hills and up bigger hills and—fuck it! I quit. I was a bodybuilder, however, so I focused my attention on that, and I still do to this day. I like bodybuilding because the only time you have to run is when you mistakenly take a laxative instead of a supplement.

We tried making a go of T's Cabaret, but the weekends were not bringing in enough business, so it was back to doing the casuals—community dances, school dances, and the Vancouver Teen Fair. Between gigs, we managed to drive down to Los Angeles, where we looked up Ike and Tina. They were performing at Gazarries on Sunset. They remembered us and let us visit them in their dressing room between shows. Ike had fond memories of Vancouver, but he had to be careful what he said while Tina was in the room. In the meantime, Tina just sat looking at us with her sexy self. She ventured a few comments about how beautiful Vancouver was, but then she had to get ready for their next set.

We got back into the car and headed north to San Francisco. We stopped at the famous Big Al's, where we inquired about work for the band. The manager invited us to catch the show that night and meet the owner, so we called up a fellow Canadian who was living in a nice apartment and begged her to put us up for the next few days. Renée was a little cutie pie I knew from Calgary. She had a fabulous job and a very nice apartment in the Nob Hill section of San Francisco.

We all piled into the apartment and made ourselves at home

in the blues tradition. That is: clean up after yourselves; if you can't pay rent, you can do chores; respect the girl's belongings and don't be in her face when she gets home from work; have a meal waiting for her; and for God's sake, keep the apartment spotless.

The weather was unusually hot and sunny so I went scouting for a place to catch some rays. I found a little spot on the roof of the apartment where I could stretch out. I was up there for about an hour when a beautiful blonde woman appeared and asked if she could join me. She, too, needed some color, and as she lay with her eyes shut, I couldn't help noticing she had a body as beautiful as her face. Blonde, Nordic, high cheekbones, piercing blue eyes. This girl was hot! So hot that when, after the tanning session, she asked where we were staying and promised to come down later and visit me, I thought, *yeah, right*! So I never said a word about her to the rest of the band.

Later that day we were watching television when there was a knock at the door. Tommie opened the door and the tan, blonde goddess was standing there, looking even more beautiful in her thin cotton summer dress. She was stunning, and the effect of her beauty was evident: No one talked. We all just looked.

"Is Tommy here?" she asked, looking around the room. "Oh, there you are," she added, as she walked toward me.

I never wanted this moment to end. The tension in the room was priceless! The guys just stood there motionless with their mouths open, one question dominating each of their minds: Who is this woman and how the fuck does she know the skinny guy with the glasses?

I smiled at the guys and escorted my new friend into the bedroom where we could be alone. She was trying to hold in her laughter as she took off her jacket and sat on the bed. She motioned for me to sit beside her and as I sat she grabbed me and laid a big, sexy kiss on my quivering lips.

She made love to me. She told me her story afterward, how she had just been dumped by her biker boyfriend, who had just been using her. She was from Germany and she owned a successful hair salon. She liked me because I reminded her of a biker and she had a thing for bikers. She talked and I listened. Listening was my specialty at the time because I could never get a word in edgewise with the guys in the band. After about an hour, she was ready to meet them. I had totally forgotten about the rest of the band and I was not eager to share my treasure with them, but she insisted and she always got what she wanted with me anyway.

The band was very eager to talk to the blonde goddess and she reveled in the attention given to her. The guys were having a hard time with the ladies in the United States. In Canada, black guys were considered special by quite a few of the foxy Vancouver ladies due to supply and demand. Back then, there were a number of football players living in Canada. Big, handsome hunks with pocketfuls of cash, all looking for a good time. These guys created a demand, and since there were only a handful of football hunks, other black men filled the void.

But we were in the States now. And in the sixties, it was impossible for the black guys in the band to even talk to the white girls at the gigs and in the clubs. I, on the other hand, was in heaven. I liked black women and we played the all-black clubs, where I would be the one guy who stood out in the crowd.

We stayed in San Francisco for a month, playing one night a week at Big Al's. The Committee, a fantastic improvisation group that featured some of the finest actors in the world, performed two shows nightly at their theater on the same block, across the street from the Jazz Workshop. I hung out at the Committee because I was really into comedy at the time, and although I was broke, I somehow managed to scrape enough money together to see them perform at least ten times. I had no idea at the time that I would someday be performing the same bits.

We headed back to Vancouver, where we were handed another club. It was a small steakhouse on Davie that had a dance hall above it. The building was owned by Jim Risbey, who owned a couple of other clubs in the city. Jim offered the club to Tommie and me free for as long as it would take to make it go, and after that he would only charge us five hundred dollars a month in rent. The club was fully furnished and the only thing we added was a small stage. We named it the Elegant Parlour, after a black magazine that was called *Elegant,* and opened the doors for business. The first two months were brutal; the customers were staying away in droves.

Tommie scored some gigs for us playing dances in White Rock, a little beach resort area close to the American border. One night I was standing at the entrance talking to the bouncer when a dream walked into sight. She was wearing a little summer dress that clung to a fine, firm body that was tanned to perfection. Tousled blonde hair framed the clearest blue eyes . . . that never looked at me even once as she made her way into the club. She was even more beautiful than the German salon owner. I was smitten. I was a wreck. I had been laid out with just one glimpse of her beauty. I turned to the doorman and said, "I want her, Pa." This was a line from a movie where a hillbilly kid sees a beautiful woman and says this to his father.

I had never in my life been so affected by a woman's beauty. And the one thing that attracted me to her was the way she ignored me. She did not look at me once when she walked into the club, I guess because I was so obvious, staring at her like some kind of pervert. I could not help myself. She had an effect on me because she was perfect. She had everything going for her in the beauty department and she had attitude up the yin-yang. That perfect nose was tilted up in a way that gave her a "hipper than thou" look. Her face was lightly covered with freckles, giving her such a youthful look that she would have gotten carded. But her body—the perfect legs, the firm breasts—eliminated any worry about her age. Her body was the ticket into any club she liked. The band started up right after she entered the club and I was given another thrill when she walked up to the stage and motioned for me to bend down so I could hear what she had to say.

"Do you know 'Walking the Dog'?" she asked in a clear voice. I noticed she did not make eye contact with me.

"Yeah, we do," I replied, staring hard at this beautiful creature.

"Well, then play it," she demanded and walked away.

I turned to the band, who were all staring at the woman and said, "Walking the Dog." I started the intro with the guitar riff I copied from the record and the band fell into the tune. It was a popular song by Rufus Thomas and it always succeeded in filling the dance floor. I searched the crowd for the beauty to no avail. She had disappeared. I spent the rest of the night thinking about her and how gorgeous she was. I somehow knew I would be seeing her again somewhere down the line because there was something about her that connected with me. Something very special. I had met my soul mate. My life partner. And even though I was married to my childhood sweetheart and had a family, everything changed when I met Shelby. Everything.

CHAPTER FIVE

A BLACK MAN'S DREAM COME TRUE

The Chitterling Circuit, 1965–1967

The Elegant Parlour was a great cash cow for more than five years. My brother, Stan, was also parlaying the cash into real estate and buying houses for all the Chongs. Maxine and I eventually moved into a house on East Fifteenth right next door to the young lady I had seen at the dance in White Rock. I was shocked to learn that the girl who prompted me to say out loud to my friend, "I want her, Pa," was my new neighbor. My little daughters, Robbi and Rae Dawn, immediately became friends with the Fiddis family. And Shelby—who was as shocked as I was at the coincidence—and her younger sister Forrest immediately fell in love with the two curly-headed, mocha-colored beauties. Eventually our families became good neighbors and friends.

Shelby and Forrest would sneak out of their house on weekends and catch a ride with Tommie and me down to the club where they would dance with the black servicemen from Seattle or with their white, hippie friends before hitting me up for cab fare to go home. It used to drive me crazy watching her dance, flirt, and sometimes even kiss her partner on the dance floor in front of me. I couldn't say anything because I was married.

Shelby would only act out when she had too much to drink and eventually she settled down and we began a love affair that is still going on today. But it was Bobby Taylor who changed everything.

When Little Daddie and the Bachelors returned to Vancouver, our drummer Floyd Sneed decided he wanted to play with another group. Floyd and Tommie were bumping heads, and the trip down to San Francisco did not produce the results we had hoped for, so Floyd decided to accept a gig with another band, leaving us without a drummer. Tommie and I then called Bobby and asked him if he knew of a drummer who wanted to come up to Vancouver and join us. Bobby did not hesitate for a second. "Yeah, I know someone," he replied, "Me." I saw a look of concern cross Tommie's face when Bobby said that he'd come up and be the drummer. We knew Bobby could play because he would sit in with Big Al's band and give the drummer a fifteen-minute break every hour on the hour. (Oh, yeah! Big Al's band never left the stage for its entire five-hour gig. Each musician would take a fifteen-minute break every hour while the music played nonstop and the girls danced nonstop. It was a grueling experience that only the young could survive. We did it one night a week and, believe me, it took at least a few days of rest to recover.) But it was Bobby's superior vocal skills that had Tommie worried. Nevertheless, Bobby came up to Vancouver and played drums for the band and, of course, sang. His presence and his voice soon had the Elegant Parlour packed with music-starved Vancouverites, who marveled at the tone and powerful range of his voice. He also attracted drummers, who would sit in when he sang so he could stand in front of the band and do his thing. Tommie, sadly, lost his job and stopped coming to the club. Tommie was a great entertainer and a good blues singer, but no one could compete with Bobby in the vocal department.

Bobby could also play a little piano and he could arrange the vocal background, which was good news for Wes, our bassist, and me. We had to step up and sing background and eventually lead on some tunes. And we could cover any tune we felt like because Bobby could sing like them all. It was sweet! Especially when we covered "My Girl," the Temptations hit written by the genius Smokey Robinson. "My Girl" was a number one hit for at least a year in 1965 and is considered today to be one of the greatest songs ever written.

We also dipped into the Impressions' songbook and learned almost every song they ever did, including a seldom-played song called "I Wonder." This was the song that we first heard Bobby sing in San Francisco and it became one of our most requested songs: "Sometimes you make me wonder . . . I get the blues and then I wonder. When you stay out late at night . . . is everything all right? Is it me? Am I a fool? . . . Sometimes I wonder." Just thinking about this song sends chills up and down my spine. Curtis Mayfield, the songwriter and leader of the Impressions, was so deep and spiritual that just listening to his songs would take people to another level. So you can imagine what it was like to actually perform them. It was very, well, spiritual. Bobby, Wes, and I would rehearse for days at a time. We never got tired of learning these great songs. Then, just before we were discovered by The Supremes and Berry Gordy, I wrote a poem that started our own songwriting career. Tom Baird, who was a talented keyboardist and composer, read my poem and put music to it. It was a poem about a black guy asking his girlfriend if her mama knew about him. The song was also about my own experiences with white women. Being half Chinese, there had been times—actually, many of them—when I had to drop a girl off at the end of the block so her parents wouldn't see who she was dating. That experience saddened me. It hurt to know that my race was a deciding factor for white people.

> *Does your mama know about me?*
> *Does she know just what I am?*
> *Will she turn her back on me?*
> *Or accept me like a man!*

Soon the Harlettes discovered the song. They were the all-girl group that sang backup for Bette Midler, Diana Ross, and Jermaine Jackson, and they actually recorded it. The lyrics also changed the way Motown songwriters wrote. Until "Does Your Mama Know About Me?" came along, R & B music had always consisted of love songs. Now songwriters started exploring the color barrier with their songs. "Papa Was a Rolling Stone" and "Love Child" come to mind as examples of this shift.

Berry Gordy loved our song, and after it hit the charts, he put us on the road with Diana Ross and the Supremes. We opened the show and performed part of our club routine, which eventually pissed off Diana Ross so much that she had the tour manager tell us to stop doing it. The part Diana took offense to was a Parliament song whose lyrics we changed to say "Oh, white girls, you sure been delicious to me." Our song pissed off the promoters, who were unprepared for an outrageous perfor-mance from the "opening act." They had hired Diana Ross and the Supremes, who had become a "white act." The promoters did not appreciate this unknown band from Canada singing about white girls' being "delicious," especially with so many white girls in the audience.

Now that I look back at this phase of our career, I realize the protest came from Diana's camp and not from the paying customers. Motown wanted to move acts like the Supremes and Marvin Gaye into bigger venues because the huge concert halls packed in monied white audiences. It was the entertainers who were trying to break the color barrier because that was where the big money was. Huge concerts made millions while little clubs made thousands. Everyone wanted the millions, especially Diana. She was the poster child for crossover music. Then again, she had the tools to pull it off. She was skinny, model beautiful, had a distinctive voice, and was going with Berry Gordy, Mr. Motown himself.

The Supremes started out as a backup singing group for the male-dominated roster of Motown singers, such as Marvin Gaye, Stevie Wonder, and David Ruffin. But it was Diana's sense of fashion and beauty that made her perfect crossover material. The Vancouvers with Bobby Taylor were also crossover material, but we were headed in the opposite direction from Diana. Our hair was getting fashionably long and our once-matching band uniforms were a thing of the past. We each dressed according to his own individual tastes. We were becoming hippies. And this was also noticed by the Motown managers.

Shelby and I were turned on to acid by a very hip lady named Helen in Vancouver. Helen was an artist-hippie-Earth Mama-heroin junkie who lived in a little shack in the mud flats on the North Shore in North Vancouver. The shacks on the mud flats were outside the building inspector's line of vision for years and were inhabited at the time by artists, musicians, and hippies. They paid no rent and they all had tiny, wooden shacks built on stilts. The shacks were connected by a walkway also built on stilts that made the living quarters accessible. The toilet was a hole in the shack floor.

Helen knew the real Mr. Tambourine Man from the Dylan song. Mr. Tambourine Man's people brought Helen some doses of LSD. She was told to "turn on and pass it around." Helen offered it to me and Bernie Sneed, my brother-in-law and piano player, but did not explain what the new drug was or what it did to you. Had she explained it to us we would not have understood it. What is there to explain? It was so new to the scene that no one really knew what it was all about. You had to try it for yourself.

We both did it and did not have to wait very long for it to take effect. Soon Bernie was in the bathroom, laughing hysterically while looking at his own reflection. I came home, sat in the garden, and watched the sun rise. I had a tremendous spiritual awakening. I became one with nature. I understood the chatter of birds. And I could hear the wind laughing at me. It was laughing in a nice way. I was so enchanted with the spiritual insights I had on the acid that I wanted to do it again.

A week or so later I tried it again, only this time I tripped with Shelby as my guide. She was the perfect one to lead me around because of the bond that existed between us. Shelby was fearless and wanted to experience life to the fullest, and although she had her heart broken by an ex-boyfriend, she felt safe with me because I was married and therefore unavailable. She could be herself around me and I could be myself around her because we were only friends. But all that changed when she accompanied me on my second acid trip.

While on acid, I realized I loved her and wanted to be with her for the rest of my life. The acid strips all the ego away and you see reality as it really is: waves of energy. These waves of energy are positive, because you realize what life is and how easy it is to appreciate every moment. We made love for the first time while I was on acid. Up until then we had only made out, kissing, hugging and touching, but we had never made love until that moment. If there is love involved, making love on acid will cement the experience in time forever. And although we both tried to pretend that we were only friends, we were only fooling ourselves.

We did try to break off the affair when Shelby left for Toronto on vacation, but she started getting morning sickness as soon as she arrived there, and when she returned, we had a decision to make. It was a no-brainer. Of course she would have our baby. Our love child. And she would come on the road with me while she carried our child. Yeah, I was married and had a family, but hey—this little boy was going to be their half brother.

Meanwhile, Berry Gordy booked the Vancouvers with Chris Clark, a very attractive, tall, blonde singer with a knockout body that aroused the beast in all the rich black men who came within a few feet of her. Berry was determined to make Chris a star even though her singing and performing skills were less than spectacular. We had backed her up in England, where we had our historical meeting with Jimi Hendrix.

Legend has it that Jimi was fired from Bobby Taylor and the Vancouvers; however, nothing could be further from the truth. Well, actually, Bobby Taylor was furthest from the truth, since he started the rumor. The truth is that after backing up Chris Clark in a theater in London, the Vancouvers scored a one-night gig in a little club called the Speak Easy in London. The club was set up as a disco, so the mic cord was only six feet long, trapping Bobby close to the mixing board. The rest of the band was situated comfortably on the tiny but adequate stage. We were playing to a crowd of about six people when the door opened, and in walked Jimi with a few hundred people behind him. We all stood there in shock, watching as Jimi approached the stage and said, "Hey, Tommy, mind if I sit in?"

Now my comic mind said, "Uh, sorry, man. We don't like other people using our instruments. But maybe you can do a number on our last set!" But in reality, I took off my guitar and handed it to Jimi. I don't think I said a word. No one had to. It was all very acidy . . . Jimi Hendrix, dressed as he was on the cover of his *Are You Experienced?* album, standing right in front of me, asking to sit in? Jimi asking me if he could play with our humble little band? Are you kidding? Here, you can have my guitar! Please, take it!

Jimi refused my offer. He wanted to play bass! Wes took off his bass and handed it to Jimi, who proceeded to put it on upside down. Jimi was left-handed and he had learned to play guitar and bass upside-down. That unusual style gave him the Hendrix sound that has baffled guitarists to this day.

I remember that we played our usual list of tunes, but I was so involved with the event taking place that I just stared at the rock god like everyone else in the club. He was mesmerizing! So beautiful, tall and skinny and dressed like an English nobleman. Peacock colors, blousey shirt, vest, boots. He was a creature from another planet and we were extras in his movie.

I don't remember the gig ending, but the club managers had to pull the plug on us or we would be still playing now. As amazing a guitar player as Jimi was, he was also a fine bass player and we all know what he could do with vocals. After the show, Bobby invited Jimi to a party in our hotel room. Of course, Jimi accepted—the party in his mind had just begun.

The hotel, however, had other ideas about a party, especially with crazy black American musicians. This was stuffy London in the sixties, in the middle of one huge cultural revolution. Scruffy young people with wild hair weren't going to get away with anything if they had anything to say about it! We were allowed in, but no one else was, especially not the underage

groupies who followed Jimi around like loyal Manson follow-
ers. Worshipping him, adoring him, just begging for a chance
to be in the same room with him or, better yet, to sleep with
him. He was the anointed one! He was the Black Prince . . . the
first Black Prince. And he wore the crown.

After our night with Jimi, we had another thrill the next
morning when we were driven to the airport in the same limo
that the Beatles used when they were in town. At least, that's
what the driver told us. We were all talking about what a thrill
it was meeting the great Jimi Hendrix when I suddenly exclaimed, "I'm going to be bigger than Jimi someday."

Ted Lewis, our drummer and main skeptic, looked at me in
amazement. "Are you serious? You think you can play better
than Hendrix?" he asked, with scorn dripping off each word.

"Not with the guitar," I said quickly. "I just know I am going
to be bigger . . ." My words trailed off into thought.

I know everyone thought I was delusional, but then again
the whole band consisted of some very strange but talented
people. Ted Lewis was certifiably nuts in so many ways, but his
drumming skills were legendary. He was so gifted that he blew
his own mind. Robbi King was on the Hammond B3. Now this
kid could play. Robbi was a classically trained piano player
from Toronto. He and Eddie Patterson on guitar were the best
and most talented musicians in the group. Our bassist and vocalist, Wes Henderson, and I sang backup for Bobby, giving the
group an Impressions-like sound that thrilled audiences all over
black America. They were all in the limo that day and they all
looked at me as if to say, "Are you serious? You? Bigger than
Hendrix?"

I have often thought of my boast that day and wondered,
*Why did I say that? Was I jealous of Jimi? No, not at all. Why
then?* I think it was because I was reading books by Catherine

Ponder, who preached that you can be whoever you want to be if you have faith in yourself. Well, I had a ton of faith in myself, so I said it out loud, "I'm black and I'm proud."

When we got back to the States, we hit the Chitterling circuit, playing all the soul venues in all the soul hotspots in the country. I had a chance to live the road life and I was living a dream. We toured with the Supremes for the month of July and rode in the bus with the band. I had a hard time sleeping sitting upright, so I found a space beneath some hanging garment bags and spread out a mattress of pillows so I could stretch out and sleep. Soon the other guys in the Vancouvers were using my little sleeper. The Supremes orchestra just rode and slept upright for the whole tour.

I was in heaven, living my dream: touring America with a soul revue. Playing legendary places like the Fox Theatre in Detroit, the Regal Theatre in Chicago, the Uptown Theater in Philly, and the Apollo Theater in New York City. The Apollo is located in the heart of Harlem at the epicenter of black culture in America. After we rehearsed our one tune, I took off on a walking tour of the famous neighborhood. I had my camera, but my first encounter with the street folks made me too frightened to point it at anyone. The sidewalk was crowded with black people of all ages, moving in all directions.

As I walked, I came across an older, skinny black man who was standing in my way, glaring at me, with a large knife in his hand. I stopped in my tracks and looked for an escape route, but before I could move I heard a commotion behind me. I turned and immediately realized that the man with the knife was glaring at another man, who was holding a guitar like a baseball bat. People around me paid no attention to this little drama but I was transfixed. I stood and stared at the fight unfolding before my eyes, until eventually both adversaries were swallowed up by the crowd. I looked around and realized I was the only one watching. *Man! This shit happens all the time around here* . . .

That night the Vancouvers were the neighborhood's latest victims. Our roadie was distracted while he was unloading our rented van and bringing our instruments into the theater. During the minute he was away from the van, thieves made off with Wes's bass guitar. This was at the Apollo Theater in New York City, and this was the welcome that it gave to all its new performers. You snooze, you lose.

However, things were quite different on the Supremes tour. We had experienced road musicians with experienced road managers, and everything was as smooth as glass. Playing with the Supremes also allowed us to travel to different neighborhoods and perform in large venues, as we motored throughout the East Coast and the Midwest from New Jersey to St. Louis. I sat on the bus and pictured the black groups of the forties and fifties who practically lived on the road, riding on buses from seven to ten hours a stretch, stopping only for gas, food, and cigarettes, and then motoring on to their next gig. I had read stories about the band bus; now I was riding and performing like many pros before me. And I was in heaven.

CHAPTER SIX

BURN, BABY, BURN

Detroit, Michigan, 1967

The year was 1967. America was having a decade-long communal barbecue. It was the time of the Ghetto Uprisings; the inner cities burned all across America. Pot was there, but instead of mellowing people out, all it did was open their eyes to the injustice and hypocrisy that was keeping them down in the gutter. Hot, sticky weather reflected the mood of the time. Hot, sticky, smelly, ghetto air hung heavy like a blanket, with no relief in sight. It was like putting a blowtorch to an anthill. People become dangerous when the heat is on. And so began the worst riots in American history. It was fight or flight! Poor folks needed attention and it seemed the best way to get someone's attention was to burn down something big! Yeah, that would wake somebody up! Or would it?

America was burning and Cheech and I were about to meet. But first I met the Jackson Five.

We were sharing a bill with Jerry "Iceman" Butler at the Regal Theatre in Chicago's South Side when we met. The Jackson Five stole the show the minute they took the stage. Michael was small for his age, which made him even more adorable, especially when he danced like James Brown. I remember the whole theater staff watching the boys from backstage, which was the ultimate compliment, coming as it did from jaded employees who saw every act and were very hard to impress. Bobby immediately invited the boys and their father, Joe, to Detroit, promising them he would get them signed to Motown. The family came, and true to his word, Bobby had them perform for Suzanne de Passe, who was Berry Gordy's right-hand woman. Suzanne saw in them what everyone did, and signed them to a seven-year contract. I know some of the details because Joe Jackson brought me the contract to look over for him. I asked Joe if he had any other offers and when he said no, I told him they would get a good education from Motown and after seven years, they would be ready for anything. Joe thanked me for my take on the situation, and his boys proceeded to step into stardom.

After Bobby met the Jackson Five, his time was devoted entirely to the kids, most notably to Michael. Bobby had a lasting effect on the Jackson family for many reasons. First he introduced them to Motown and Berry Gordy. And Bobby could relate to the kids because they were similar in many ways. One example: they were all raised by strong, God-fearing Christian mothers. Plus Bobby had full control over the guys because he could outsing all of them, even Michael.

But the Jackson Five quickly grew out of Bobby's control and soon other people at Motown were producing the hottest group of kids in the business. America could not get enough of this talented family, and a wild time was had by all—except perhaps Michael. I felt it was as if Michael really became an adult when he was ten years old. That was when I first met him and he was an innocent kid with the most fantastic voice I had ever heard. But I think he was beginning to realize, as the rest of us already had, that he was special. His singing was light-years ahead of anyone else in the business, young or old. And his moves onstage exceeded even his dance teachers' tutelage.

They usually ended up taking a lesson from the little master. All the Jacksons were polite, well-mannered, and extremely focused on their act.

By the time Michael came of age, he had done it all. The only thing he had never done was have a childhood. So, like so many rich and successful men before him, Michael set out to manufacture his own version of childhood.

I remember watching other members of Motown go crazy with their newfound wealth, spending money on crazy shit. Exotic animals were the fad for some time. You could buy wild animals from Africa—lions, tigers, ferrets—as house pets. Chris Clark kept an ocelot in her hotel room and Bobby bought a young male lion and kept it in his apartment in Detroit. He loved the looks on other tenants' faces when he got into the elevator with his lion on a leash.

At that time, Detroit was still recovering from the riots, and its streets were far from safe. Yet Shelby would take a bus and go downtown to the department stores that were located right in the heart of the riot-torn city. She was a sight to behold, a young, pregnant white girl standing in the ghetto waiting for a bus. She never got hassled! Not once! She was so innocent and pure that I don't think people even thought she was real. She seemed like a ghost standing there.

I enjoyed my time in Detroit because it was not only happening music-wise, but also comedy-wise. I had the honor of seeing Redd Foxx at the Twenty Grand nightclub. This was Redd at his finest—and dirtiest. Redd did two hours that night. He brought people to the point where we physically could not laugh any more. My sides were aching. He stood on that stage and rattled off joke after joke until tears rolled down my face, and then he would abruptly shift gears and talk politics, ragging on whoever was in charge, ripping them to shreds to the point where people got up and left because they were so insulted by his off-color comedy. I was worried that he had completely lost the crowd. They were turning on him fast. But then Redd reeled off a series of side-splitters that earned him a standing ovation at the end of his act.

To this day I can repeat almost verbatim Redd's act from that night. The only bit he did not do was "My Dick," his famous racetrack routine, in which he names racehorses after various body parts: "My Dick followed closely by Wet Towel . . . with Middle Finger coming up the rear." I first heard this bit on a dirty record we found in an army dump near our house in Calgary. It was the first comedy record I had ever heard; Redd had a big influence on me right out of the gate. Comedy was really my first love, even before music. I would always choose it over music whenever I had to make a choice of which kind of show to see. I remember being in Chicago and having to choose between seeing a stellar lineup of blues legends and seeing Second City, and I chose Second City without hesitation. But as much as I loved comedy, I never in my wildest dreams thought that I would end up being a comedian . . . until the cracks began to form in my relationship with Motown Records.

Bobby was eventually lured away from the Vancouvers toward the end of 1968. In addition to producing the Jackson Five, he recorded a solo album called *Taylor Made Soul*, featuring the Smokey Robinson penned "Melinda," which gave him a minor hit. His solo career freed us up to work with other artists, so we went on tour again with Chris Clark. Our first gig was at a club in Cherry Hill, New Jersey, and I brought my girlfriend Shelby and our brand-new baby, Precious, on the road with me. When we landed, Wes and I found out that we had to attend an immigration hearing on Saturday and wouldn't be able to make the gig. Chris Clark was quite annoyed when I announced this new development and brooded throughout the rehearsal. "Why can't you postpone the meeting until we get back?" she asked, though it was more of a statement than a question. So I tried to explain the U.S. Immigration facts of life to her: "We can't postpone the meeting because they called the meeting and told us if we miss this meeting we will have to wait up to a year to get another." *Goddamn it! Get your no-talent head out of your ass and listen to what I am saying!* I didn't say that last part but I sure thought it. We went on with the rehearsal, but everyone was still pissed and nothing had been resolved.

Wes and I left bright and early Saturday morning for the most important meeting of our lives. We were about to become legal, green-card-holding residents of the United States. No more fear at the U.S. border. No more waiting for the "knock" at the door. (You can always tell a cop's knock—it's hard and unyielding and definitely unsympathetic.) And now I would never have to fear that knock again . . . or so I thought. (See page 26 of *The I Chong: Meditations from the Joint.*) Wes wasn't as thrilled as I was. In fact, he was questioning whether he wanted to live in the States at all. His wife and two little boys missed Edmonton, Alberta, and I could see that Wes missed home, too.

We showed up at the Immigration office, we were hustled through a brief question-and-answer session about the history of the United States, and that was that. It was over and we had passed the test. I felt so good that I wanted to celebrate, but Wes was a little dark and moody; he wouldn't even make conversation with me. I sensed his need for privacy and I backed off. That afternoon, I called Motown for tickets back to Cherry Hill and was told there was a ticket for Wes, but not one for me.

That's strange, I thought. *Maybe they just forgot. Who knows?*

there was a place in his company for me. I thanked Berry for his support and I thanked him for understanding my role in the band. And then I told him that I had to leave the group because I wanted to become a Berry Gordy myself and I had to do that on my own. Berry paused to take in what I said, and then he told me he understood and wished me luck.

Later that week, Shelby and I went to see *I Love You, Alice B. Toklas,* starring my favorite comedic actor, Peter Sellers. The movie featured a group of hippies who take a straight business-man and turn him on to the joys of free love and pot brownies. It was a complete departure from previous Hollywood movies, which always portrayed the long-haired hippies as deranged dope dealers or bikers. It was also the first and the best of the hippie movies because it showed the love and the gentleness of pot culture. Its positive message stayed with me for years. I saw my future in that movie. I saw the direction in which I wanted to go. I saw who I wanted to be. It was so clear to me: we had to go to California. Why not? I was free to do whatever I wanted. No more band. No more Motown. Just me and my families.

I had heard of a program in which people hire drivers to take their cars back to the West Coast, so I called them up, and within a few days, Shelby, Precious, and I were in a brand-new Oldsmobile and on our way to Los Angeles.

Maxine had a job and the girls were in school in Detroit, but I promised to send for them as soon as I got settled. Maxine actually liked living in Detroit. She had never been in a situa-tion where the majority of the city's population was black and she liked the vibe. She and the girls were staying on a beautiful, tree-lined street, surrounded by friends who had grown up in the area. The rest of Detroit, however, was dangerous and still smoldering from the riots.

Shelby, Precious, and I arrived in Los Angeles via San Diego and drove right to the beach. Unfortunately, we were still miles from our destination, Venice Beach, but we didn't care. We were in California and we could see the Pacific Ocean; this was what we had come for. Yahoo! California. The weather was gorgeous compared with Detroit's. The sun was shining and the surfers were strolling around in short-sleeve shirts, while the girls wore summer dresses that showed off their legs. California seemed like heaven.

We finally found Venice Beach and checked into a motel on Lincoln Avenue near Navy Street. I noticed a Honda motorbike dealership across the street from the motel and went shopping for a Honda 90. It was the motorbike of choice for the population of South Vietnam. The evening news would feature thousands of South Vietnamese people moving their entire belongings and family on one Honda 90. The bike was durable and could hold two adults and a child, which made it perfect for us. I had to drive to Palm Springs to deliver our drive-away car to its owner and then return on a Greyhound bus. I tried to load the scooter into the trunk of the car and ride the scooter back, but luckily the bike didn't fit or else I'd still be stuck out in the desert somewhere with no gas, trying to get back to town.

My next plan was to join the world-famous Gold's Gym, started by Joe Gold so his friends would have a place to pump iron. I had read about the gym in many bodybuilding magazines and was looking forward to becoming a member and meeting all the bodybuilding stars. The ride to the gym was my first attempt at driving a motorbike and, of course, I fell off. But that was my one and only fall during the five years I rode it, so it wasn't so bad.

I arrived at Gold's Gym and met the manager, who told me, "Membership is thirty dollars for three months, no instructions, and you can come as many times as you like. Don't leave your shit unlocked and put the weights back when you are finished with them. That's it." I recognized the guy at once from the magazines—he was the famous "Mr. Abs" himself! Zabo Koszewski, the chief. His claim to fame was that he won hundreds of bodybuilding trophies with a body that was untouched by steroids. He was the poster boy for the joys of "natural" bodybuilding. He did, however, have an alcohol problem, and he smoked a ton of weed, but other than that, he was Mr. Natural. I started working out that night and, despite his "no instructions" rule, as soon as Zabo saw that I did not know what I was doing, he showed me a good basic routine that I use to this day.

The next day, we found a one-room apartment on the beach, at the corner of the boardwalk and Venice Avenue, for eighty-five dollars a month. It was small and located in the rear of the one-story complex, but it was so close to the beach that it made sense. All we wanted to do was go to the beach and enjoy the beautiful California sunshine.

The first morning I was awakened by a tap on the window. I opened it and was greeted with a hand holding a huge lit joint as the sweet smell of California grass wafted through the room. The hand disappeared once I had possession of the enormous joint, so I took a toke and immediately put it out to save it for later. Moments later someone knocked again. I opened the window and a long-haired hippie appeared smiling. "Did you enjoy the 'welcome to California' smoke?" Before I could answer he went on, "Hey, we are on our way to a concert in New York, wanna come?" I smiled at the suggestion of leaving California

to go back to the cold weather and politely declined the invitation. Man, nothing could have gotten me off the beach and
back into cold northern weather. I didn't care that I was missing the famous Woodstock concert. I was in sunny California
and I was here to stay.

Or so I thought.

I called Maxine every day, checking in with my first family
like a good husband because I was worried about leaving them
in Detroit. Although Maxine was enjoying the cultural aspects
of living in an all-black community, it was still Detroit, and
anyone with sense would have gotten out of that hellhole if
given the chance. Maxine's brother Floyd, who was doing quite
well as a drummer and a founding member of Three Dog Night,
was living in Los Angeles with his family, in an apartment complex on San Vicente west of La Brea. The building was located
in an upscale, middle-class neighborhood close to schools, and
there was an apartment available. It was perfect for Maxine and
the girls. So they packed up and made the trip. I was thrilled to
have them with me again—and thrilled that I didn't have to
feel guilty about being in Los Angeles without them. Robbi
and Rae Dawn were happy because they had their cousins
Tracy and Shannon to play with. Maxine scored a job right
away that enabled her to get the girls into school and keep a
roof over their heads. I was giving her what money I could, but
she was really the breadwinner during this time in our lives.
Once again I was scooting back and forth between my two
families every day.

As hectic as it was, I was very content with my life because I
was with the people I loved. But although I was living my
dream, I knew I had to do more. So I looked within myself and
started asking for instructions. I needed a goal. I needed answers. So I followed the advice of the Scriptures—ask and ye

shall receive. I asked. I would lie quietly in the sun and ask for help. "Please, show me the Way." And again according to Scriptures, I was shown the way. It was the way back to Vancouver with Shelby and Precious.

The clubs needed me and I needed them.

CHAPTER SEVEN

A NEW LIFE, A NEW WIFE

Vancouver, British Columbia, Canada, 1968

My mom and dad were shocked when I showed up with Shelby and Precious. They had no idea Shelby and I were together and no clue that we had a baby. Of course, Mom and Pop fell in love with Precious immediately. But they loved Maxine like a daughter and were sad to see that I had fallen out of love with her and in love with Shelby. Yes, it was confusing, but hey! I was a black man in those days and that was the kind of thing we did. I needed Vancouver more than I needed Los Angeles. And Vancouver needed my craziness, so it proved to be a good move. The Shanghai Junk and the Elegant Parlour were being operated by my brother, Stan, in my absence. He was the boss, but I was the brains.

My welcome back to the clubs in Vancouver started off on the wrong foot when the door staff at the Junk would not let me in because, with my long hair and wire-rim glasses, I looked like one of those troublemaking hippies. I pretended to be a customer just to see the ticket girl's reaction. It was quite funny when she finally realized who she was telling to go away. I also pulled a prank over at the Parlour by sitting at the "owner's table" with a couple of regular customers, who took half the night to finally recognize me.

I began working the lights during the girls' show. It was pretty basic Bada-Bing-type stuff, where the girls would each do two or three numbers—a fast one, a slow one, and a medium one, taking off their clothes as they danced. The girls were quite young and had great, firm bodies and real breasts. Silicone had not yet arrived in Vancouver. It was "Silicone Valley" big-time in San Francisco, but in Canada, we had to settle for real titties that bounced and sagged and came in all shapes and sizes. I, for one, was quite happy with the real thing. But the show itself lacked so much. Even the die-hard perverts had a hard time watching some of the girls. So while I sat and worked the lights, I wrote a show for them.

These were young, sexy, beautiful women who turned heads when they walked down the street fully clothed. They did not need to wear skimpy clothes or pile on makeup to look sexy; in fact, they looked much sexier without it. When they walked into the club wearing tight blue jeans and sexy tops, they looked like the girl next door, and everyone wants to fuck the girl next door.

So I wrote a little play in which the girls would pretend to have a pajama party in their apartment after doing a show at the club. As the girls arrived, they all had to undress and put on their pajamas. Normally when the girls disrobed onstage they did it to music. You know the routine; it was the same shit every strip club in the world was doing. But watching girls undress and put on baby-doll pajamas can be quite an experience, especially when they do it as if they are alone in their own apartment.

To top off the girls' pajama party, Jeanne, our singer, performed with Taps Harris, our dancer and emcee. The first show was a resounding success—Tap's dancing was so well received that he did an encore. Everyone was buzzed with the club's new vibe. Everyone, that is, except Taps, who quit the show the next day. "Man, I am too old to be doing this shit," were, I believe, his exact words. So I asked Dave the doorman if he wanted to step in, and he looked at me and said words that would change my life forever: "Yeah, I'll do it if you do it with me."

Until that moment I had not even considered being in the show, but before I knew it I was writing it, directing it, and acting in it. Dave Graham was the star of the show, and he named the group the City Works. Dave was and still is a minor legend in Canada. Born in England, Dave was raised in Edmonton and worked behind the scenes at a jazz club called the Foggy Manor. He was married to Toni Gerry, a beautiful, hip, black girl from Edmonton. I knew her through Gail Lewis—my ex-fiancée and my daughter Rae Dawn's mother—before she married Dave.

Now that Dave, the girls, and I were cast, we needed a straight man. All the improv groups I had seen had a couple of straight-looking actors, and because both Dave and I had very long hair we needed the contrast to give the group more versatility. Rick Lenz was a character actor and magician who came onboard as our resident straight man. And we also added the great classical guitarist, Gaye Delorme, who would, of course, eventually write the music for Cheech and Chong's biggest musical hit, "Earache My Eye."

The moment I changed the strip show into an improv show, word spread through the acting community like wildfire, and within hours, actors were lining up to audition. The bits we did were embarrassingly simple—the only rule was that the punch line had to include a girl taking off her clothes. Dave and I did a couple of the Committee and Second City bits that I remembered from my travels with the band, and true to the spirit of improvisation, we ended the first half by taking suggestions from the audience for the second half. Of course, the early audience would leave before their suggestions were acted out, but that never bothered us because we were having so much fun, and the new audience would never know the difference. When we first started the improv, the opening bit tended to upset the audience. We never really made a formal announcement about changing the format of the show. So the audience—made up mostly of lonely, sex-starved, horny men—came to the club expecting to see the strippers' usual bump and grind and got something quite different.

Picture a group of working-class guys—fishermen, longshoremen, truckers, a good number of mean, grizzled bikers—and a sprinkling of suits, all watching the stage waiting for the young ladies to appear. Instead of the girls, they get a classical guitarist and a mime. That's right: the show opened with a white-faced mime doing a silent routine about finding a flower in the park, all set to a beautiful classical guitar piece.

Needless to say the audience is watching all this incredulously with open mouths. A few of them would start heckling the mime, but most would just sit there as if in a trance. As the mime would leave the stage, Dave would enter, dressed in hippie garb, wearing a cowboy hat and scarf, and would sing an ode to his puppy in classic chamber music style, accompanied, of course, by the guitarist. After a beat, I would kick the door open—messy, shirtless, and half asleep—and ask Dave, "What kind of fucking song is that?" before beating him on the head and shoulders with a rolled-up newspaper.

And that always brought down the house! Rick the magician loved doing the show. He always played the straight man because he looked like a cop—short hair, horn-rimmed glasses, a bit on the pudgy side. But his wife gave him an ultimatum: either quit or move out. So, sadly, Rick had to quit the show. I immediately started looking for another straight man to fill his role. Quite a few people applied, but none really fit the bill.

The show attracted Vancouver's hip crowd and with them came hash, weed, and acid. And with the drugs came the undercover cops. The Parlour on Davie Street was closing because the building had been sold, so I moved the club into a room behind the Shanghai Junk. Shelby and I scoured the junk stores for old pictures and things to give the place a hippie atmosphere. This turned out not to be such a good idea; although it attracted hippies, it did not attract the Parlour crowd, who were about as far removed from hippies as one could get. They were the night people—gangsters, hustlers, pimps, hookers, and drunk businessmen out on the town. The last place they wanted to be was in a hippie joint. But hey, I was a hippie and it was my club, so I thought, *fuck 'em all if they don't like it.*

The day of the official opening, I was busy mopping the floor and putting the finishing touches on the back room when a couple of visitors stopped by—a man and a woman, dressed in blue jeans and looking a little out of place.

"So what's going on here?" the guy asked in a friendly but somehow weird manner.

"Just getting ready for tonight's opening," I replied and kept on mopping.

"Oh, we don't want to bother you," the man answered, as the woman looked around the club with a practiced eye. She was casing the joint pretty seriously. *Hm, what do we have here?* I thought.

"So we just got into town and, uh, do you need help?" he asked.

"Do I need help?" I replied, thinking, *Now, this is weird.*
"Naw . . . I just have to mop up a bit."

"We'll help you," he replied, taking the mop from my hands.

The woman started lifting chairs onto tables and within minutes they had the place sparkling clean. Moving deliberately from chore to chore, they were like a well-oiled cleaning crew. We took a well-deserved break and I treated everyone to a cold soda as we sat in a booth admiring their hard work.

"So how long have you had the club?" the guy asked.

"A couple of years," I replied.

"You get a lot of customers?" he asked.

Now I started to get really suspicious. *What the fuck is going on here?* I wondered. "Yeah, we do all right. The neighborhood is a bit rough, but we do all right."

"Yeah, lots of drugs in the neighborhood, I bet," he looked at me hard as he sipped his drink. The woman was quiet, still sweating from the work. Her eyes were darting around making mental notes as she sat there.

"So you guys into drugs yourself?" I asked, knowing the answer. These guys have never done drugs. I doubt if they even smoked cigarettes.

"Oh, yeah, we do a lot of drugs," he replied.

Cops. These guys are cops. My brain was screaming at me.

"How about acid?" I asked, trying to keep my voice from giving away my true thoughts.

"Oh, yeah, we do acid. Don't we, babe?" he said to his partner, trying to get her into the conversation.

"Yeah, we do acid," she replied, sounding a lot more like a cop.

"So tell me . . . what was your first acid trip like?" I asked.

"Our first acid trip? You know, I don't remember," he answered, falling headlong into my verbal trap.

He doesn't remember his first acid trip? You can forget your name, but you will remember your first acid trip. You always remember the first time you got laid and you always remember your first acid trip. That is, unless you have never done acid! Fucking cops. Fucking undercover cops! And here they were cleaning up my club for me. How sweet is that?

"Well, we better get moving if we are going to open on time tonight," and I put the pigs back to work for about another couple of hours, putting tables and chairs in their places, while I pretended to be busy looking at guest lists and bar supplies. I wanted to call someone and tell them that I had me some undercover cops slaving away while I watched, but there was no one around, so I had to enjoy the party all by myself. They finally left with a promise to be back for the opening later that night.

The place started filling up around ten P.M. The undercover cops arrived early and sat in a booth facing the door in the main club. The back room the cops had cleaned would not open until after midnight, so they sat in plain view. I had tipped off the doorman, who in turn tipped off everyone who he knew needed tipping off, and soon the cops were completely isolated in their booth. All drug sales in the club were suspended in honor of our out-of-towners, and for a brief period, no one in the Shanghai Junk was ripped on anything heavier than a beer or an overpriced cocktail. The cops, who were probably fresh out of the Saskatchewan Police Academy, eventually picked up the vibe and left before midnight, when the club they had worked so hard to clean officially opened.

We closed the old Elegant Parlour, marking the end of an era at a place that had been like home to many nightlife people and that had hosted some legendary musicians in its day. But the hippie thing was taking over and the dancing and rhythm-

and-blues featured at the old Parlour gave way to laid-back music for a laid-back crowd at the new, cop-cleaned Parlour behind the Shanghai Junk. We had musicians from Edmonton play there—a group called Django (after the legendary French Gypsy guitarist), featuring Canada's own legendary guitarist, Gaye Delorme, who played with the City Works and was the best blues and jazz guitarist I had ever heard. And I had heard a few in my time. Gaye was so good that he made me put down the guitar and concentrate on comedy. Whenever Django played, the plan was to get ripped on weed and acid and then sit back, munch on shortbread cookies from Chinatown, and groove to the fantastic music.

We were out of business within two months.

It's hard to make money when your customers are too stoned and too broke to buy even a cup of coffee. There's no money in hippies, believe me. But there are other things more important than money, and I was realizing more each day that acting with the troupe was what I really wanted to do. I found joy in acting the likes of which I had never before experienced. The freedom and control was addictive and the more I did it, the more I looked forward to doing it again and again.

One day, a guy who had been coming to the club quite regularly—a Russian named Ihor Toduk—approached me about a young guy who he thought would make a great addition to our troupe. Ihor owned and operated an underground newspaper and invited me to the farmhouse out in Richmond, British Columbia, where he published it, to meet this would-be straight man. I borrowed my dad's car and Shelby, Precious, and I drove out to meet him.

He introduced himself as Richard, looked very straight, and was extremely well-spoken. Richard showed me his desk, where he was working on a music review. I noticed that he was copying material for his review straight from an issue of *Rolling Stone*. *Hm, so this is how one reviews bands*, I thought. After the meeting, as we drove back to Vancouver, Shelby asked me, "What do you think of the new guy?"

"Well, he is a straight man, that's for sure."

I had this feeling, though, that I was somehow involved in something very important. Richard wasn't what I had expected, but then again, I had no idea what to expect. He promised to come and catch a show as soon as possible and then decide whether he wanted to be involved. I thought it was a little strange that he said he was going to audition us first, but hey, I liked that cocky approach.

There was something about the little guy that had me thinking about him as we drove back to civilization. A few nights later he showed up with a beautiful woman on his arm— a beautiful, rich woman dressed in a full-length mink coat. She had dark hair and looked like a character out of a crime novel. Richard's stock immediately rose because I had learned many years ago from the pimps, hos, and gangsters that you could judge a man by his woman. The hotter the woman, the smarter the man. The guy could be short and funny-looking, but a tall, gorgeous woman has the power to make him look hip.

And that night, Cheech—or Richard, as he liked to be called—looked six feet tall.

CHAPTER EIGHT

DAVE WAS HERE

Vancouver, British Columbia, 1969

Richard liked the show, joined the group, and became the understudy for Dave and me. Over the ensuing weeks he grew his hair and mustache and soon he was as hippie-looking as the rest of us. He had told us he had been in an improv group in the States, but we later found out that that lie was his first attempt at improv. It didn't matter to me, though; the club was packing them in and we were kicking ass.

I came from the world of the blues, where we spent a good deal of time learning the licks and lyrics of the great blues players before us. This is how music survived for hundreds of years. You learned licks, and the great ones would show you their licks so you could then show someone else. And the only way to stop anyone from copying you was to do what Coltrane eventually did. He got so damn good that no one could copy him! Not when he was alive. The blues is a tradition that needs to be passed down to the next generation. And I feel that comedy falls into the same category.

A good joke is supposed to be shared, passed around. The good ones are told and retold to spread joy. Joy has to be shared to exist. I went down to Los Angeles to visit Maxine and the girls and I caught the Committee's new show while I was there. They were even funnier and fresher than they were in San Francisco. They did a bit where the entire cast got down on their hands and knees and started acting like dogs, sniffing one another's butts. One even pretended to take a dump on the stage while the others went over and sniffed the finished product. I thought it was hilarious.

I stayed after the show and met the director. I told him about our group in Canada and suggested that we arrange for them to come up there and work. I noticed the director's eyes glaze over as he talked to me and realized he must hear guys like me at every show, so I shut up and left.

When I got back to Vancouver, I told the City Works group about the dog bit I had seen the Committee do, and we came up with a variation for our next show. It brought the house down. People were laughing so hard, they fell out of their seats. Man! What a feeling! Making people laugh so hard they fall over is such a nice rush . . . even though we were using someone else's material. But I didn't even think about it at the time. A laugh is a laugh. But we got lots of flack when we started making records. And what comes around goes around. A lot of people copied Cheech and Chong, too.

Eventually, our success brought about a financial problem that we could not overcome. Although the club was packing them in, it was losing money. The crowd had changed from a small group of hard-drinking, easy-tipping perverts, to a wine-sipping, no-tipping theater crowd. Unlike the horny men who used to spend a fortune at the bar and tip the sexy dancers well, the new Parlour regulars spent little money and left immediately after the show. This was a classic example of being ruined by success. The better the show got, the more intelligent the crowd became. And intelligent, straight people tend to count their change and drink very moderately, unlike free-spirited bikers, who tend to throw their money around at every opportunity.

After one very successful, packed-house weekend, Stan gave me the bad news. We had to go back to the old strip show or risk going under. It was costing money to service the packed houses and even if we raised the door fee, we would still be in the red. I looked at my brother as he stood there holding a stack of unpaid bills and I felt relieved. I wasn't sad or angry in the least. The show had peaked and the run was over. My time in Vancouver had again determined the course of my career, and although I did not know it at the time, I was pointed toward a new goal in life, a goal that I knew I would attain.

The City Works actors were actually relieved by the news as well. The girls, who were getting less and less time onstage, would once again be the stars of the show. Dave was about to quit because of his health. His knees got so beat up doing the dog routine that he could hardly walk. So he was happy. Richard never really expressed his feelings one way or another—I guess because he, too, was ready to move on to the next adventure. As for me, I wasn't ready to quit the stage, and although I knew the improv group was history, I felt there was something waiting for me around the corner.

The City Works performed one more time, at the request of Three Dog Night, who were performing at the arena in Vancouver. I had known the drummer—then my brother-in-law—Floyd Sneed, ever since he was ten years old. I even gave him his first gig, playing bongos in a band I had formed when I was back in Calgary during the early sixties. When they asked us to perform, Three Dog Night was one of the biggest rock bands in the world and were on a world tour. Floyd was showing them Vancouver, and when he found out about the Shanghai Junk, he brought "the Dog" down to catch a show. I gathered up the gang and we did a command performance in the back room of the Junk. The guys loved the show, and Danny Hutton, the unofficial leader of the group, invited us to look him up when we got to Los Angeles. I smiled at the invitation, and for some strange reason, I had a feeling that I would be seeing Danny in Los Angeles.

Richard and I started talking about forming a rock-and-roll band. Talking music again was comforting; however, I was still humming from the rush of performing with the City Works. The difference between being a musician and an actor is that you play music but you become an actor. I didn't know it at the time, but I had become an actor.

Instead of looking around for musicians to use in my new band, I just waited for them to show themselves. It seemed that the harder I tried to do something, the harder it was to make it happen. On the other hand, the more I allowed things to happen on their own, the faster they happened. A tall, bearded bass player was the first to make an impression on me. His name was Tom Lavin, and he looked like an undertaker: He dressed all in black and even drove a hearse. This was the sixties, when everything was weird, so although the car was perfectly legal, he was routinely stopped by the police. But he was prepared for that. He had all the paperwork on a clipboard—insurance papers, vehicle title, driver's license—so the police could run their customary background check and then he would be on his way. Tom, who eventually went on to form the Powder Blue swing band and built a successful recording studio, helped us put the rest of the band together. I don't recall the names of the others in the band, but I do recall our first and only gig.

I still had my reputation as the blues guitar player with Bobby Taylor and the Vancouvers, so when word got out that I was forming a new band, we were immediately offered a gig by a local promoter. We were to be one of the bands in a Battle of the Bands at the Gardens, the local hockey rink/concert hall, where I had performed with Tommie Melton. I had only one rehearsal with Tom Lavin and the boys. We stumbled through a couple of tunes and sounded like the worst band I had ever been involved with—in this lifetime, anyway.

But the show must go on, so when the night of the gig came, we were set up and ready to play. I told the guys that Rich and I would go out and warm up the crowd with some comedy, and then we would play (or attempt to play) the tunes we rehearsed. Rich and I performed all the bits that Dave and I used to do, to gales of laughter. One bit melted into the next until we ended the show and had both forgotten entirely about the band sitting behind their instruments, waiting to play. After the band had collected their instruments to make way for the next act, Tom Lavin came up to me and asked, "Well, when's our next gig, boss?" I looked at Tom and saw the glint in his eye and I laughed out loud. That was the funniest line of the night.

Later that night, when Rich and I were alone in my pop's car, driving through a big rainstorm, we went over what had just happened. We had become a comedy team. A duo. Just the two of us. The rain pelted the windshield and we could hardly see the road. That was partly because the windshield wipers didn't work. In fact, they had never worked. Imagine driving a car without windshield wipers in Vancouver, a place where they get approximately two hundred inches of rain every twenty-four hours! Well, that's just what my truck-driving dad did; he had a system worked out. He carried a bent wire clothes hanger that he would wrap around the arm of the windshield wiper so he could work it by hand, while driving. And that is just what we did, too, except we took turns leaning out into the rain and get-

ting soaked trying to clear enough window so we wouldn't
drive off the road.

"Man we kicked ass tonight! You did Dave's part better than
Dave!"

"Well, I guess its you and me, baby."

"What are we going to call ourselves?"

"Let's think about it . . . Chong and Marin?"

"Naw."

"Richard and Tommy?"

"Hey, don't you have a nickname?"

"Yeah . . . Cheech."

"Cheech and Chong."

"Yeah, I like that!"

"Cheech and Chong. Nice!" I stuck my head out into the rain
and as I wiped the windows with the coat hanger washers, I
screamed out into the wind and rain, "Cheech and Chong . . .
Cheech and Chong!" Man, it felt good screaming our name.

The next day I was on the phone, looking for clubs where
we could work. Now that we had an act, we wanted to get back
onstage as soon as possible. I wanted to perform in a club that
I did not own or have anything to do with—I just wanted to be
the act. So I called an old friend, an American singer I had the
pleasure of working with over the years at the New Delhi. Ronnie Small, along with his wife Shirley, owned and operated a
little folk-blues club on Davie Street across from the Elegant
Parlour. Ronnie was kind enough to let us perform between his
music sets.

As luck would have it, the musical talent was the legendary
T-Bone Walker—Mr. "Stormy Monday" himself! I had the thrill
of seeing Mr. Walker play at a tiny folk club to a small but eager
crowd when he was at the top of his game . . . and what a game
it was. Besides being a fabulous guitarist with a repertoire of

thousands of jazz and blues standards, he was also a physical wonder. T-Bone played a special performance at the New Delhi (our club) when he was in his prime. This was the performance where he did the back bend with the guitar behind his neck, picked up a glass of whiskey with his teeth, and drank it while coming out of the back bend into the splits, still playing the difficult jazz tune "Body and Soul." I had to see it to believe it and believe me I saw it.

One night, Cheech and I watched as the great legend was led onstage. It was quite obvious that he was drunk, falling-down drunk. T-Bone was so drunk they had to put the guitar in his lap and place his hand around the neck of the instrument. Then he came to life and started strumming; however, the strings had been loosened for the flight and were flapping around like rubber bands with each drunken stroke. The drummer picked up the rhythm and started a beat, while the bass player tried to tune T-Bone's guitar while he was playing it! T-Bone then started muttering some drunken, unconnected words, thinking that he was singing. I stared at this spectacle in awe.

The scene was hilarious, but no one was laughing. I looked around and the crowd was staring at this inebriated legend like he was a god. The crowd was actually buying this comedy of drunken slurs. The untuned guitar added a bizarre effect to the drum and bass, sounding more like avant-garde, new age, African noise than music. But when they stopped playing, the crowd erupted in applause and shouts of, "Bravo!" I felt like I was on some kind of nightmare acid trip. Are they really applauding this wreck of a man as he stumbles and slurs unintelligible lyrics? Yes, they are. In fact, some people even gave T-Bone a standing ovation.

Cheech and I both found the whole scene with T-Bone hilarious. Years later, we put a version of what we saw that night on our first Cheech and Chong album, only instead of T-Bone we called the character Blind Melon Chitlin'.

But more important, we were happy with our show and we were ready to take it back to Los Angeles.

CHAPTER NINE

BACK TO L.A. AND THE QUEST FOR FAME AND FORTUNE

Los Angeles, California, 1970

Shelby wasn't exactly jumping for joy at my decision to go to Los Angeles and live with Maxine while Cheech and I toured the comedy clubs. And Maxine was not exactly jumping for joy either at the prospect of two unemployed comedians living at her house. But we had no other choice.

Cheech and I moved down to Los Angeles and stayed with Maxine and the girls. Maxine was very gracious, but she did not understand my decision to change careers and become a comedian. My daughters were just glad to have their crazy dad home again, and I enjoyed the hell out of that part of the new living arrangement.

However, I was in love with Shelby and I knew it showed. Things were not the same between Maxine and me. There was so much tension that Cheech contacted a couple of his long-lost L.A. buddies and left for Lake Arrowhead to stay with them. Cheech had been sleeping on the couch and getting very little sleep because Robbi and Rae Dawn, ages six and ten, would wake him up every morning while they ate their cereal and watched cartoons. (We actually used that scene in *Up in Smoke*.)

Meanwhile, I lost no time connecting with some people I knew from my music days, including Redd Foxx, who is, in my opinion, the greatest comic of all time. Redd was so far ahead of his time that he could truly be called the van Gogh of comedy. Van Gogh never received recognition for his art until after he was dead, and then the rest of the world caught up to him. Well, it was the same with Redd Foxx. His humor and insights were as hip and sharp as anyone on the scene today, yesterday, or tomorrow. Redd could blow Eddie Murphy, Richard Pryor, Chris Rock—you name it—off the stage at any time. I know I just named the best of the best, but I believe Redd was the role model who everyone in the business has to try to follow. I still do.

Redd owned a comedy club on La Cienega, where he had open-mic night every Monday. Redd was performing out of town, but the club manager, Norma Miller, told us to come down Monday and show her our act. When Cheech called that night I told him the good news, but he didn't respond like I expected him to. He was a little hesitant because he had just gone out to Lake Arrowhead and now he had to come back to do the club. I felt a twinge of panic. Was Cheech going to punk out on me now, before we even gave the act a chance?

But Cheech showed up and we went over our set list before the show. When we arrived at Redd's club, ready for our first Los Angeles appearance, there were more comics standing around than customers. But one table caught my eye because they looked like customers who went to my club in Vancouver— tough-looking, streetwise people. Norma Miller was the emcee and the only real pro in the room. Norma was famous back in the day for her jitterbug dancing, and now she was honing her comedic skills, talking shit about each comic after they did their five minutes.

Cheech and I did a couple of routines ending with a funny mime of a guy brushing his teeth. While he brushes his friend says, "Hey, have you seen my Preparation H? Oh, there it is." and snatches the imaginary tube from his hand. Laughs . . . and we exit the stage.

As soon as we got backstage, a tall, skinny, good-looking Chicano greeted me with a handshake and a compliment about the show. I smiled and said thank you and he invited me outside to talk. He introduced himself as Tony Bruce, Lenny Bruce's father-in-law.

"You are Lenny's father-in-law?" I asked, sizing up the guy.

"It's a long story . . . Hey, you guys are good. How long have you been doing this?"

"About a year," I replied, still trying to figure out how Lenny's father-in-law would have the same last name that he did.

"Well, you guys are the closest I've seen to Lenny since he died. I'm with his people now. Come on, I'll introduce you to them."

We walked back into the club, where we gathered up Cheech and joined Tony and his crew. "This is Sally Marr, Lenny's mother, and Jo Jo, his road manager," and Tony went down the line, introducing us to the gang who used to follow Lenny from club to club. Tony and I talked for about an hour while Cheech talked to the rest of Lenny's support group. As his mother and unofficial adviser, Sally was the biggest and loudest laugher in his audiences. You can hear her voice loud and clear on some of Lenny's early records. Comics need people at their shows who laugh because laughter is infectious and good laughter can turn a poor show into a good one.

Tony was very excited to meet us. He finally fessed up that

he was not a Bruce. He was, in fact, a Vascaria. Tony Vascaria, ex-hairdresser, roadie, heroin junkie and comedy writer. He married Sally Marr back when Lenny was just beginning to make it. Sally and Tony both lied to each other about their ages. She was fifty and said she was forty, and he was eighteen and said he was thirty. They got married, went on a honeymoon, and separated when they returned, but they remained very close friends right up until Tony died of a heart attack in 1981.

Tony became a very close friend. He gave me advice about comedy, honest advice that helped me to no end. I loved Tony for many reasons. He had a comic's eye. He could see the funny in every situation. He had been involved in gangs when he was a kid, until he went into juvenile detention for accidentally shooting another boy in the ass. According to Tony, he had been chasing the kid with a zip gun, a homemade weapon that fired a single shot. Tony claims he tripped and the gun went off when he fell hitting the guy in the ass with a .22 slug. Tony had been in minor scrapes with the law prior to the ass-shooting, so he was sent to juvie, where he learned how to box and how to do hair.

He got out of juvie hall and secured a job at Douglas Aircraft. Eventually, he tired of the hard physical labor and opened his own hair salon on Sunset, where an actress named Marilyn Monroe became a steady customer. Tony knew a lot about comedy, so when he offered to manage us, I said yes immediately. I thought, *Hey, what do we have to lose?* But when I told Cheech, he was less than enthusiastic. I thought the Lenny connection would be enough to get us to the right people, but our new manager turned out to be a little less than I had hoped.

To begin with, Tony had a heroin habit. And Lenny Bruce had a heroin habit. I had a feeling that Lenny turned Tony on to the deadly drug, but I wasn't sure. It could have been the other way around. Tony told me he was the last person to see Lenny before he died—that he was the one who gave Lenny his last heroin shot, the one that killed him.

Still, I liked Tony, and he appeared to have his habit under control when he started working as our manager. In addition to securing a couple of open-mic gigs, he also took me along to scout some clubs that offered floor shows. The first club we visited wasn't suitable for comedy, and as we stood outside talking about the venue, a white customer came up and started a conversation. I was about to answer the guy when Tony said in a low voice, "Do I know you?"

The guy looked at him and answered, "No, I don't think so." Tony then said, "Then get the fuck out of my face."

The guy did not hesitate; he just walked away. I looked at Tony with a great deal of respect. His eyes were hardened by years of tough living. He had been through a rough childhood and old habits die hard. Tony explained a few days later that nobody starts up a conversation with strangers for no reason. He could have been a cop. Or just a square. Either way, you don't waste time with fuckheads like that.

That night I came back to Maxine's apartment and discovered I had lost my wallet. Could that guy have been a pickpocket? Could be. I told Maxine the next morning and she reacted in a way that really surprised me. She asked me to leave. Actually she *told* me to leave. She said to take my stuff and get out of her house. She stopped short of acknowledging Shelby, but for her, our relationship was over. Losing my wallet was the straw that broke the camel's back, as well as our marriage.

Maxine and I both knew I was in love with Shelby, and I knew that Maxine had lovers when I was away with the band. We had grown up together and she had always been the straight girl in my double life, but that had been when I was a working musician and supported her. Now I was without a job and without a prospect of a job, so I had to go.

Shelby and Precious were living in a motel in Venice when Maxine threw me out of her house. I took my one bag of clothes, got on my Honda, and scooted over to my new life. I felt an enormous weight lifted off my shoulders. I was free! No more lying, no more feelings of guilt, no more strained conversations.

Maxine really was, and still is, a saint. She is the most decent, beautiful woman I have had the privilege of being married to. And we have remained friends to this day. She gave me money when I was dead broke so Shelby and I could eat. She loaned me her car whenever Cheech and I needed to go somewhere. And once, she took care of Precious while Shelby was in the hospital. I loved Maxine when we were together and I will always love her.

Ironically, Shelby had come to L.A. to break it off with me. She was tired of my double life. But when I arrived with the news that we could finally be together officially, she fell in love with me again. We found a little one-bedroom cabin on Fourth and Pico in Venice for rent at eighty-five dollars a month. It was one of a group of three summer cabins built there in the thirties and forties. They were surrounded by a six-foot wooden fence and situated in a fairly nice neighborhood. The cabin reminded me of the one I grew up in in Calgary, except that this one had indoor plumbing. I asked my brother, Stan, to wire me the rent money and a few bucks for some furniture and we moved into our new home.

Our neighbors were two brothers who had turned their cabin into an art studio. They were friendly hippie types, but they got really tired of letting me use their telephone. My daughter Robbi called me constantly. She called when she got up and she called when she got home from school, and every time she called, the neighbor had to stop what he was doing to come get me. I apologized every time, but I couldn't tell my little girl not to call me. Rae Dawn was hurt the most when I left because she was old enough to understand why, and I guess she must have felt abandoned. And this was after I had gone to court years earlier to get custody from her mother, Gail. It was sad, but hey, no one said life was supposed to be without pain.

The brothers next door did get a little revenge for my excessive phone use when they talked me into buying a water bed from them. The only trouble with the water bed was that I did not know it needed a frame. Shelby and I had to sneak up on it to lie down on it, or it would just slosh over to the other side of the room.

By this time, my clubs in Vancouver had both closed—the building that housed the Elegant Parlour had been sold and the topless, mindless dancer shows at the Junk weren't pulling in enough profit to sustain the place. I was left with no income, and once again, Shelby, Precious, and I were homeless.

We had to leave the cabin for reasons other than the rent. Most of our gigs were in West Hollywood, which meant a long-ass scooter ride from Venice at night in the cold. Also, Shelby hadn't had much luck making friends among the other mothers in the neighborhood. She befriended a Chicana lady—a tough, street-gang girl, complete with tattoos and shaved eyebrows, who lived across the alley with her baby boy. One day, she attacked Shelby because of some drug-induced notion that our daughter Precious had hit her baby. Shelby was shaken to the core and when she told me about the attack, I knew we had to move.

We had been working at a club on Sunset called Kanopos Steak House, where we would do shows once a week in exchange for meals. The pay started out with steaks, but they soon were downgraded to hamburgers. One of the waitresses, a gorgeous redhead named Barbie, took a liking to Cheech and within a couple of days, he had moved into her one-bedroom apartment on La Jolla in West Hollywood.

Shelby flew back to Vancouver with Precious and stayed with her sister, while I moved in with Cheech and Barbie. Cheech was cool about this new arrangement, but I could tell Barbie was less than thrilled, so I tried to stay out of their way. Barbie had access to a garage workshop where I would spend time whittling away. I made candle holders from wine bottles I scrounged from the garbage. I also carved wooden hash pipes, a habit that eventually landed me in jail. I used to work out in the garage until everyone had gone to sleep; then I would quietly come in and sleep on the couch. The arrangement would have worked out had it not been for one cold night when the temperature fell to zero. Too cold to work in the garage, I came into the apartment a little early. Cheech and Barbie were in their bedroom, and I lay down on the couch and settled into a deep sleep. I was awoken a couple of hours later by the glow and heat of flames that were shooting out of a space heater. A cushion had fallen on the little-used heater and had caught on fire. I screamed and jumped off the couch. Cheech appeared within seconds and we managed to smother the flames with a comforter. It was an accident, and Cheech was pretty cool about it, but Barbie wasn't. I don't blame her; I almost burned down her apartment. Barbie was also getting flak from her parents about Cheech. They did not approve of her living with an unemployed Chicano, and they would show their displeasure in various sneaky ways, such as her father referring to Cheech as Chimp—"Is Chimp with you, dear?"

The final straw for Barbie was when Shelby and Precious arrived and we all had to stay with her and Cheech. Barbie went out bright and early the very next morning and found us a duplex that was for rent on the corner of La Jolla and Santa Monica. I think she even helped us move our stuff.

Things were getting pretty desperate for Cheech and Chong. Even the weather was against us. I remember riding my scooter in cold, sleet-like rain to pick up Shelby and Precious at the airport. The ride to the airport in that mess was bad enough, but now I had to pick up my girl and my daughter and motor all the way back. Shelby hopped on the scooter with Precious snuggled between us, and we got all the way home before we realized that we forgot Shelby's suitcase! I had to motor back in the fucking rain to retrieve it from the baggage area. That meant four trips in the freezing rain that night. I can still remember how wet and cold I was. I remember pulling up to stoplights and looking at the other drivers, warm and snug in their cars while I shivered on the scooter beside them, thinking of a future when I would be the one in the warm car. I still remember that feeling today, and I give thanks every time I sit in a warm car when it's cold outside. Well, maybe not every time, but I do appreciate the comforts in life and I smile when I hear my kids complain about things.

While my family settled into our new apartment, Cheech and I played every club we could. We were getting within reach of the brass ring, but it seemed the closer we got, the more broke we got. All the clubs were within scooter distance now and we were hitting them frequently. We appeared somewhat regularly at P.J.'s. The wannabes who owned the club liked Cheech and me because we used to do gangster bits such as the one in which an undercover cop got busted by a little Chicano dealer he was trying to bust for pot. The club booked big-name jazz acts like Carmen McRae and Cannonball Adderley, and we would open the show for them.

The audience was mostly made up of black pimps, hos, and thugs, with some middle-age jazz lovers mixed in. They all came to see the floor show, featuring strippers, comics, musicians, and vocalists. This was an era when the musicians smoked reefer with the strippers and the vocalists between sets, the entertainers honed their comic skills by sparring with a very hip audience, and the pimps, who had cash to throw around, tipped the waiters well so they would turn out-of-town businessmen on to their girls, who would show the guys a good time.

Comics like Lenny Bruce, Redd Foxx, Moms Mabley, and Lord Buckley worked these clubs; they made you laugh, but they also made you think. It wasn't about how many dirty words you could use in a show. It was about what those words were telling you. The Troubadour on Santa Monica was the best club for exposure. They had a Hootenanny Night every Monday, where the acts would have to sign in to determine the order of the performances. For instance, if you signed in first then you would go on sixth. The sixth spot was the best, because by then, the club would have customers. The first few acts would sometimes just play for the staff.

We liked the sixth spot so we would get to the club by nine AM and we would wait until six PM, when the box office opened and we could sign in. Cheech and I would stand around eating sunflower seeds until we were knee-deep in empty husks! But it was worth it because all the top acts not only performed there, but also hung out in the bar. Every night you would see music legends like Janis Joplin, Mick Jagger, and Joni Mitchell at the bar or on the stage. Doug Weston, the owner, would have the acts sign a promise that if they made it big they would still play for scale. All the acts signed without complaint. But before I tell you about the Troubadour, I have to tell you about the club that changed our career forever.

The Irma Hotel was a dance club located in Reseda on Van Nuys Boulevard. It was run by a guy named Slippery John. This was the era of the long-haired hippie peace-love-dope thing, and John was all that. The club, however, was in the Valley, and it catered to dancers. John had seen us perform at another club in Topanga and loved our act. He thought our comedy would be great for the Irma Hotel and hired us to play weekends for at least a month.

Cheech and I showed up in our Goodwill costumes, prepared to kick some comedy ass. We were surprised when our show was not well received. Bit after bit fell on unloving ears, and by the time we finished the first show, I knew we were in trouble. Afterward, Cheech and I sat in the dressing room and plotted our next move. This was like the intermission at the Junk in Vancouver, when we tried to figure out what to do with the suggestions from the audience. Yeah, we had suggestions from the audience that night, too, and the suggestion was, "Go home."

"Hey, man . . . you are from here—we need a character they can relate to . . ."

Cheech looked at me with a serious expression because he knew, as I knew, that we bombed.

"Well, there is one character, but . . . it's a lowrider," he replied.

"What's a lowrider?" I asked.

"He's a Chicano character, but I don't want to do him," he replied, looking even more serious.

"Why not?"

"Because it's detrimental to the Chicano community," he blurted out, with passion I had never seen before.

"I don't understand . . . Is he funny?"

"Yeah."

"Well, let's do him. What does this lowrider do" I asked, getting into my writer's mode.

"He is into his car. He is like a gangbanger except he is really into his car."

As Cheech explained the ways of a lowrider, a bit was forming in my head and we worked out a sketch. Cheech would mime cleaning his lowrider, and then he would get in the car and give the audience a sense of what the interior looked like. He would then drive away cruising for chicks until he spotted a hitchhiker, and then he would stop the car and holler, "Come on, baby, I'll give you a ride."

That was my cue to appear onstage out of breath, as if I had been running, and then I'd get in his car and comment on the interior in my stoner voice. "Oh, wow, man. I like your car, man."

"Oh, yeah, man? I did it myself," Cheech would say, all proud of his work.

"It looks like someone threw up in here," I replied like a stoner.

"Hey, don't talk about my car, man. You wanna get out and walk?"

"Whoa . . . What's that?"

"Oh, that's my plastic Jesus."

"I thought it was a hash pipe."

"Yeah, it is a hash pipe, man. See, you smoke out of his feet."

Then Cheech would mime taking off at top speed. "First gear . . . second gear . . . third gear." I would be thrown back in my seat, hanging on for dear life.

"So how far you going, man?"

"The end of the block would be fine."

"Hey, you ain't afraid of a little speed are you, man?"

My demeanor would change from scared to very interested. "You got some speed, man?"

"Uh, no, I ain't got some speed, but I'll tell you what I do got. Here, check this out, man," as he hands me a tiny joint.

"Oh, wow, this looks like a toothpick. Hey, man, it is a toothpick."

"Uh, wrong pocket . . . oh, yeah, here it is . . . no, that's my dick . . . ah, here it is . . . fire that sucker up, man, and prepare for blastoff."

When the bit ended we received the loudest applause we had gotten in our entire career! Cheech and I stood on the stage and smiled at each other. We had climbed another mountain and only had a few hundred to go.

The next week we showed up at the club and noticed our name had been taken down. *That's strange*, we thought. A new manager greeted us and informed us that Slippery John no longer worked at the club; therefore, we no longer worked at the club.

"But he hired us for two weeks and we haven't been paid yet . . ." I protested.

"Well, come into the office and we will settle up." We followed him as he led us into his small office.

"So you worked last week and how much did he promise you?"

"Uh, two hundred dollars. Each."

"Well, you didn't work this week," the manager replied as he handed us two hundred dollars.

"Hey, we said two hundred each," I said.

"Yeah, I know . . . Thank you and say hi to Slippery John for me," he said and walked us briskly out of the room and onto the street.

We looked at each other and laughed at my clumsy attempt to squeeze money out of the guy.

"Slippery John told us he owned the club," I said laughing. "And we believed him . . ." Hey, if you can't laugh at your own fuckups, what right do you have laughing at other people when they fuck up?

P.J.'s was always in the news because the club was constantly getting robbed. It happened like clockwork. The robberies would only take place when the safe was full of weekend cash. So Cheech and I always asked to be paid right after our show, knowing that the chances of getting paid after the robbery were very iffy.

I was never very good with money, so when I found out that Shelby had special business powers, I used her brain to make all my decisions. And doing that was the best decision I ever made. Barbie was supporting Cheech at the time—paying rent and buying the food and nagging him to get a job. She understood his quest to be a successful comic, but she was also trying to become an actress and saw no reason why he couldn't hold down a day job as well. Cheech did what he could to supplement her income, like using his writer's credentials to get major record companies to send him free records to review. Cheech would then sell them at used record stores or trade them for products he wanted. Cheech also used to write to large food companies complaining about their products and would receive complimentary products in the mail days later.

Eventually Barbie gave him an ultimatum—get a job or get out. It was the same at my house, only Shelby wasn't supporting me. She tried to find work as a waitress but no one wanted to hire her because she looked too young. Like Cheech, I, too, had run out of cash cows. My brother quit sending me money when the clubs went under. Maxine had her hands full supporting herself and our two daughters, so I couldn't go to her anymore.

It was crunch time in the Cheech and Chong households. I still remember the conversations very clearly.

"Listen, I need some new shoes," Shelby said, awaiting an answer. "Are you listening to me?"

"Yeah, I hear you."

"Well, what are we going to do?"

"Uh, I'm thinking."

"Well, think up some money because if you can't buy me new shoes I am going back to Vancouver to live with my sister until I get a job."

"So you have a plan?" I asked, not knowing what else to say.

"Well, we have to do something. Precious needs new clothes, I need—"

"Shoes. Yeah, you told me. Well, let me go to the bank and see where we are here." I knew I did not have any money in the bank, but it was just around the corner and it was a good reason to get out of the house. I never was one for confrontation. I run away from my problems, which is why I left Vancouver to go to Detroit, and why I left Detroit to come to L.A., and why I left the house to go to the bank. I am not at my best when I am confronted with money problems. That was the main reason why I wanted to make it so badly. I did not want to deal with real problems. I wanted fantasy. I wanted make-believe. I wanted to just entertain and have people laugh at my silly ass. Confronting me with problems takes the edge off my high.

As I walked the couple of blocks to the bank, a strange feeling came over me. I felt a little excited for some reason that I could not put my finger on. It was a feeling of anticipation, not one of anger, despite the mini-fight I had just had with my love. The bank was empty when I approached the teller. She smiled and said, "What can I do for you today?"

I smiled back and thought, *Give me all your money now. Put it in this bag and don't make a sound.* The teller waited for my answer so I handed her my bankbook and inquired, "Will you check and see how much I have in my account, please?"

The teller came back a minute later and handed me the book and a sheet of paper with the number $2,000 written on it. I stared at the sum and asked, "Uh, this is what I got?"

"Yes, is there something else I can do for you?"

"Uh, yeah . . . I would like to withdraw . . . five hundred dollars, please."

The teller proceeded to fill out a withdrawal slip, which she had me sign before counting out five hundred dollars. I don't remember walking home but I do remember walking into the kitchen and saying, "Will this be enough for your shoes?" as I handed Shelby the money.

"Where did you get this?"

"From the bank."

"I thought we were broke."

'So did I, but when I asked how much was in the account she handed me this."

Shelby took the slip of paper with the balance of two thousand dollars and studied it for a while. Then she counted the five hundred. "There is only five hundred dollars here."

"I know. That's all I took."

"Well, go back and get the rest!"

"Go back?"

"Yes, go back and get the rest before they find out they made a mistake! Go! Hurry!"

I left the five hundred with Shelby and went back to the bank and I approached the same teller.

"So, back for more?" she asked, smiling.

I almost bolted for the door but I steadied myself and mumbled, "Yeah, I just realized I need the rest of the money in my account. I got bills . . ."

The teller filled out another withdrawal slip that I signed in a hurry. This time she disappeared for quite a while, leaving me in a pool of sweat as I tried to formulate a story in case this was a setup or something.

She finally appeared with my cash in hand and proceeded to count out fifteen hundred dollars in new crisp bills. I tried to walk out of the bank in a normal, unhurried manner, but I was skipping as I rushed outside. I did it! Then I started to worry. *This is not my money,* I thought. *But why was it in my account? And why am I holding it now? Yes, it is my money. It was a gift from God. That's it! I was stone-cold broke and now I have two thousand dollars. Thank you. Thank you. Thank you.*

Shelby was waiting for me when I walked in the door. "Did you get it?" she asked in a breathless, excited manner.

"I got it. I got it all, baby!"

"We better hide it." She was thinking ahead. She was the practical one in the relationship. This was why we made a good team. I brought the money home and she hid it.

"We can't hide it here. They might search the house."

"Why would they search the house? It's my money. They gave it to me."

"Hide it over at Cheech's." Cheech and Barbie lived two blocks down the street on La Jolla. So I hustled over there and knocked on the door. Cheech opened the door, shirtless and looking like he had just woken up from a nap.

"Here, hide this for me." I shoved the money into his hands. He looked at the bundle of cash for a second.

"Where did you get this?"

I told him the story and he disappeared into the apartment with the cash in his hand. I went back to my house and started painting the front room. Apart from the beds and dressers, our apartment was empty of furniture. We did have an inflatable chair in the middle of the living room that had a slow leak and had to be pumped up periodically. The duplex was a wonderful old two-story clapboard, *Leave It to Beaver* kind of house, with a full-grown avocado tree in the backyard. Our neighbors were a university professor, his wife, and their two grown hippie sons. The sons worked at an incense factory, so the place smelled of sandalwood and pine. Our place had a great fifties-style kitchen, a dining room, a front room, and two bedrooms upstairs. The empty rooms showed off the beauty of the house but also showed how badly it needed painting. Personally, I thought the place looked fine, but then again I am just a writer. For some reason, being messy and unorganized seems to make me more comfortable. I think it's because we writers seldom really finish a project. Our manuscripts are taken from us by force by our editors, who then have to tidy up after us. I have yet to meet a tidy writer, except for Harold Robbins. I met him at his estate on Mulholland and it was super neat and tidy, although I never saw where he did the actual writing.

As Shelby and I gave the living room walls a new paint job, we found ourselves jumping every time the phone rang. We didn't answer it all day. We tried to concentrate on the painting, but every little noise spooked us. I had to make a run to the paint store to buy more supplies, and by the time I returned, the phone had stopped ringing and we relaxed and enjoyed a nice meal with an expensive bottle of wine.

But at seven AM the next morning all hell broke loose. We woke up to find the walls shaking and the ground rumbling. It felt like a freight train was passing by right next to the house. It was an earthquake, the 7.1 Sylmar quake, which lasted almost two minutes! In an earthquake, a minute is an eternity, especially if it's your first, and we were scared. The furniture in the bedroom was jumping around and you could see the walls undulating, as the earth pulsed up and down like waves in an ocean.

I stumbled to our daughter's bedroom and picked her up. She was sound asleep and started to cry when I grabbed her from her bed. "No . . ." she cried. She did not want to wake up. Precious was an independent little girl who did not like to be picked up unless she requested it. She was three, but she had already walked to the corner store, where she purchased some candy and then walked home all by herself. This freaked people out when we told them, but we were from Canada where we kids walked to the corner store every day without fear.

The quake finally subsided and we listened to 1070 AM, the all-news station, with a shaken announcer telling us what we already knew. An earthquake measuring 7.1 had just hit the Los Angeles area. The epicenter was said to be in Northridge, California. The announcer went on to describe the damage while we walked outside, where the neighbors had gathered to re-count the event and survey the destruction. Our house came through the event unscathed, so within an hour we were back inside, painting the dining room. The earthquake happened on a Saturday. The banks were closed on Sunday, but bright and early Monday morning we heard the anticipated knock on the door. Shelby dropped her brush and scurried up the stairs, leaving me alone to answer the door.

It was the bank manager and his assistant. He introduced

himself and walked into our house uninvited. His assistant walked in behind him. He was a heavyset man in his forties and he looked like, well, a bank manager: rimless glasses, neat haircut, a Republican poster child. I smiled and waited for him to begin the conversation. He cleared his throat and began with "I assume you know why we're here."

"Why don't you have a seat," I replied, offering him the blowup chair. He sat down and looked at me. I waited for him to continue but he just stared at me, waiting for an answer.

"Uh, no, I don't know. Why are you here?" I replied.

"Well, you have money that doesn't belong to you. Our money."

"Your money . . . I don't have your money," I countered.

"Are you not Tommy Chong?"

"Yeah."

"And did you not withdraw . . ." he paused while he looked at a sheet of paper in his hand. "Two thousand dollars from your account?"

"Uh, yeah. Last Friday. Yes, I did," I replied.

"Well, the teller credited your account by mistake—"

I cut him off, "Oh, that's what happened," I replied, sounding relieved as if a great mystery had been cleared up.

"Well, Mr. Chong, I am sorry to inform you, but that money does not belong to you," he shot back with his mean coplike voice.

"Hey, she gave it to me, man! She insisted I had the money in my account, and she helped me write out the withdrawal slip. I did not steal the money," I said in my mean victim's voice.

"We are not accusing you of theft, Mr. Chong, but we would like our money back," he said with a hint of pleading in his voice.

"Well, I don't have it," I replied. I wasn't lying. The money wasn't in my possession.

"Then where is it?" he asked.

"I spent it!" I said with conviction. "I had a shitload of bills due, which is why I went to the bank . . ."

"What made you think you had money in your account?" he asked, as he struggled to get out of the chair that had him trapped.

"I don't know . . . I thought I would just look and see how much I had."

"Do you know how much you had in your account?" His voice rose as he tried in vain to free himself from the grip of the inflatable chair.

"No," I replied. "That's why I went to the bank."

He cut me off this time. "You are five dollars overdrawn . . ." His face reddened as he tried to get up. "Help me, for chris- sake!" His assistant was trying to pull his boss out of the chair, but all he succeeded in doing was to stand him upright with the chair stuck to his ass. The assistant and I looked at each other and we tried not to laugh. The bank manager was getting livid. His face was red and I was beginning to fear for his life. *He might have a heart attack,* I thought. I finally pulled the chair off his fat ass, and as they prepared to leave, he turned to me and asked again, "What made you think you had money in your account?"

It was a good thing I had been studying improvisation be- cause I did not skip a beat as I answered in my most sincere voice. "You know, I don't know. For some reason I felt com- pelled to go to the bank and when I saw my balance I immedi- ately assumed the record company had deposited the money directly into my account."

He looked at me and asked, "What record company?"

"Motown Records," I replied looking him straight in the eye. "I am a writer for Motown Records and since they owe me money I thought they had to be the ones."

"So when are you going to return the money?" he asked as they headed out the door.

"Just as soon as I get the check from Motown," I replied. I gave them a nice "thanks for coming but get the fuck outta here" smile and closed the door.

Shelby came down the stairs immediately after they left and I told her the good news. A few hours later I walked down to Cheech's house to retrieve the cash. He greeted me with the news that he had spent six hundred on a lawyer. He found a lawyer who would make it right for him to be back in L.A. He had dodged the draft, but when he went down to the draft board and showed them his injured leg from a skiing accident, they immediately listed him as 4-F, and now he was free.

I retrieved the rest of the cash and pulled a classic Tommy Chong. I bought an old '67 T-Bird that belonged to our neighbor, for twenty-five dollars. They offered it to me free but I insisted on paying something. The car had been parked in their driveway for a while because the motor was completely shot. Everything else worked and I thought I had scored big-time. It was a classic T-Bird, for chrissake!

This was my argument to Shelby when she inquired about my state of mind. I immediately found a company that installed used motors at an incredibly low price and had the car towed there. Two weeks later, Shelby and I picked it up and drove about a mile from the shop before it died. I had been scammed. Shelby just looked at me like a wife looks at her dumb-ass husband who makes the same mistakes over and over, and shook her head. One would think that I would know better, but unfortunately that was not the case.

I am an old-car junkie, and I have been since birth. I was car-deprived when I was growing up. My dad always came home with so-called bargains, old cars that barely ran. I can remember sleeping in the back of a 1929 Chevrolet and seeing the ground through the holes in the floorboards.

My dad did score a beautiful 1941 Buick Roadmaster four-door sedan with a straight eight engine. We kept that car for ten years! I learned to drive in the big Buick and after I got my driver's license, I would borrow it and take dates to drive-in movies. I never got laid in that car—I guess because I was always behind the wheel and more interested in driving than fucking, if you can believe that. The straight eight motor gave the car incredible power but it also burned a lot of gas. Luckily, gas prices were seventeen cents a gallon, so I could purchase a dollar's worth of gas and be cool for the night.

I once acquired a rare 1933 Plymouth three-window coupe. I was just fifteen years old, still riding a bicycle, and was delivering meat for the local butcher. I saw the old coupe parked in an empty lot with weeds growing all around it. When I inquired about it, the lady told me to take it if I wanted it. I had my brother help me tow it home, where I parked it in my backyard. It was a beautiful but neglected coupe that had "freewheeling" transmission. I had no idea what that meant because I was and still am mechanically challenged. I just liked the way it looked.

My fiddle-playing mentor, Mel, was over at our house some months later and got excited when he saw the car parked in the backyard. "Where did you get it?" he asked. I told him the story, and before I knew it he was bent over the motor fiddling with something. I peered over his shoulder and looked at the motor for the first time. Mel smiled at me and said, "Let's get this baby running."

I was stunned. My car ran! I thought it was just going to sit in my backyard for the rest of its life. But within an hour Mel had the car purring like a kitten, the motor running smoothly on all six cylinders. Man, this was too cool—my car actually ran!

However, I was only fifteen years old and did not have a license. But I drove the car anyway and enjoyed the thrill of a three-window coupe with free-wheeling transmission that allowed the car to coast along without transmission drag. My biggest problem was money. I never had the bucks to fix it up properly or to even buy the license plates or insurance. So after one glorious day on the open road, the car remained parked at my house until my mother gave it to another bright-eyed car lover who showed up to inquire, just like I had.

CHAPTER TEN

OH, LORD,
HOW MUCH LONGER?

Los Angeles, California, 1971

We had been struggling in Los Angeles for almost a year, and I was ready to own my own nightclub again. Struggling with a steady income is far better than struggling without one. For one thing, a steady income quiets the wives. Women are more likely to allow a man to go his own way if they are allowed to buy anything they want. I have always said that a woman with a purse full of cash and credit cards is happier than one who has to dust around a lazy stoner who doesn't have the energy to even flush the toilet or take out the garbage.

So when Doug, a friend of Cheech's, informed me of an empty nightclub less than two blocks from my apartment, I immediately walked down the street to check it out. There it was, tucked neatly between a dry cleaner and a steakhouse, a perfectly viable nightclub, complete with tables and chairs, bars, and bathrooms, all there and ready to go.

When I inquired about the place from the owner of the steakhouse, he hugged me as if I were a lost relative. He was Al Gilbert, a legendary restaurateur who owned steakhouses and hot dog stands all over Los Angeles and Palm Springs. Al was a throwback to the Al Capone Chicago gangster days of the thirties. He wore a hat and drove an El Camino, and the whole time we worked on getting the club into shape, he entertained us with his gangster stories.

According to Al, the club was empty because the last operator didn't know squat about the nightclub business. "You boys look like you know what you're doing. Just listen to Al and I'll make you rich," he would say. The truth was, Al never listened to anybody. He would make you think he was listening, but then halfway through your story Al would think of something else and cut you off mid-sentence to tell you his thoughts. He had wisdom, though, and I listened with glee to his stories and to his philosophy.

Al had a brother who worked at one of his hot dog stands on Santa Monica. The brother was really too old to work in the extremely hot stand, but Al would say to Cheech and me, "He blew all his money and I am not supporting the guy. So he has to work. Hey, we all have to work, right? You're working, right?" We would not respond, but would listen to Al intently as he went on about not supporting the whole goddamn city. Lazy bastards want handouts.

Al showed us how to scam restaurant supply companies out of equipment by telling us to load equipment into his El Camino while Al kept the guy busy arguing over an overdue bill. The guy would not notice his equipment until we were driving away. Al would laugh and say, "The guy thinks he can overcharge me? They hike the price up three or four times and they think I don't know? I've been in this business for many years and I know how much they pay for this shit. They pay nothing. And they get upset when I even the score a little."

Cheech and I worked our butts off getting the club ready to open. We named it the First Stage, intending it to be a starting point for comics and singers trying to get into the business. I drew a crude but effective sign on plywood, and we attached it to the stand that was already on the roof of the building. I made candleholders out of empty wine bottles and pieces of plywood. I had been working in Barbie's garage workshop making stuff for sale, and now we had a place to put my hippie art. The design was simple: I would cut the bottles in half and fill the top half with wax and a wick. It was a design I saw in an old army fort near Calgary. The back of the candleholder would have a picture that was cut out of a magazine and glued on and covered with clear Varathane. They were easy to make and they fit in with the hippie culture that we were very much a part of. We lined the walls with the candleholders, put traditional glass candleholders on the tables, and the place was ready for business. The only thing we needed now was an audience.

What could we do to get a crowd in Hollywood? The answer came to me that night when I suddenly awoke from a sound sleep. I jumped out of bed and started writing down the idea that woke me up. A movie. We had to make a movie of the opening! We didn't have to actually make a movie; we just had to act like we were making a movie and advertise for actors. Aha! Just like the City Works. Improvisation. That was the answer. So I called up the *Hollywood Reporter* and placed an ad in the classified section. *Wanted: actors and actresses for nightclub scene. Auditions will start at 2 PM.* I gave the address, and that was that.

In the meantime, Cheech and I attended a Chicago concert, where we heard a killer group called Mudera. They were a three-piece rock and jazz group that just burned! Their killer song was an up-tempo version of Chuck Berry's "Johnny B. Goode." When we heard that song we knew we were listening to a group that would set the music world on its collective ear. They were not only good musicians and singers, but also looked the part.

Their hair, clothes, attitude—everything worked. So we added them to the show at the First Stage.

The day finally arrived and I immediately received a call from the manager of the steakhouse, who informed me the place was a madhouse. It was only 9 AM and people were lined up around the block waiting to audition for our "movie." I hung up the phone and before I could move, another call came in; this time it was a cameraman who was inquiring if I had a camera crew. I never really intended on having a camera crew. I just wanted people to fill the nightclub for our show. I was only interested in getting an audience. So I told him the truth and instead of hanging up, he offered his services free! I couldn't turn down an offer like that, so I said welcome aboard, Mr. Cameraman. He also told me he would provide a sound man and the film. He was using his 16 mm, so the film cost would be minimal. I said bring it on! Let's shoot this baby!

Cheech and I arrived at the club around noon and started interviewing the actors. We brought them in one at a time during the first few hours; then we had to bring them in three and four at a time as the line grew longer. We told the actors that they were playing an audience in a comedy club. They had to pay for their own drinks, and because this was a super low-budget film, no one was getting paid a dime. In exchange, they were getting a first-class comedy and music show that they would remember for the rest of their lives.

The great thing was that almost everyone went along with the plan. A few of the pros saw through the scam and left immediately, but most stayed and watched the show. I was completely unaware of the cameraman, but he and his one-man crew were busy cranking out the footage.

Showtime at the First Stage. The band Mudera started the show and did their killer set. The audience responded, but because they were actors and not real music lovers, they responded in a more subtle manner than the audience at the Chicago show. But still, they loved the opening act. Now it was time for the stars of the show, direct from their apartments down the block. "Ladies and gentleman, please welcome the owners of this little nightclub here on beautiful Santa Monica Boulevard. Give it up for Cheech and Chong!"

We walked onstage to thunderous applause and went into the act. Everything was clicking along smoothly until Cheech went into his "Right-on Washington" routine. This is the bit where Cheech enters the stage wearing his *Shaft* outfit—a ridiculous afro wig and a blue jumpsuit with high-heel shoes. He walks in saying, "Right on. Right on. Right on. Power to the people," and other black slogans that were all over the movies and television at that time. Usually this bit killed the pimps and hos at P.J.'s, but someone in the audience started heckling Cheech, who just kept on and didn't miss a beat. Right-on Washington finished his bit by introducing me as Blind Melon Chitlin', an old, drunk, fucked-up blues player who was too wasted to perform.

I was doing our version of T-Bone Walker, but before I even got into the act I started getting heckled. It was weird, because this bit usually killed audiences wherever we went. I ignored the catcalls and went on with the show, and at the end we got a standing ovation from our actor audience.

Shelby was working as one of the waitresses, serving drinks as fast as she could. We had another girl from Vancouver working as the other waitress. "Did you hear Nina heckling you guys?" Shelby asked, as she cleaned up the tables in the club.

"That was Nina yelling at us?" I asked. Nina was a friend—or so I thought—from Vancouver. She had been involved with my ex-brother-in-law, Bernie, and was a nice-looking white girl who loved black guys. Shelby and Nina were the hottest waitresses in Vancouver during our time there. Both of them made at least a hundred dollars a night in tips, which in those days was a fortune, considering I made only five dollars a night and I was part of the draw.

"What was her problem?" I asked. Shelby was too busy with her tables to find out, so I went over and asked Nina directly.

"Your show is a disgrace to black people," she replied. "I can't believe you guys, especially you, Tommy. You are married to a black woman. How could you be so insensitive?"

I saw right away why she was so upset. This was her first exposure to the cutting-edge humor of Cheech and Chong; had she known what we were all about, she would not have worked the gig. And if I had known how she felt, she would not have been allowed near the club. I was pissed off, not because she was offended by our humor, but because she worked the club and kept making money while she was being offended. That black-power bullshit always pissed me off because I had listened to black comics sticking it to the white people for years. And now, just because we were giving it back to them, we were insensitive disgraces? We did this act in front of big-name pimps and they all laughed at the humor. Black people never came up to us and gave us the shit that Nina, a white girl from Canada, gave us. Black people understood humor that depicted them in a humorous manner. Right-on Washington was funny! And besides, Cheech isn't white! He is Mexican! He has every right to get them back, considering all the Mexican jokes that black comics have used over the years.

It was such a weird night—playing to a packed house in front of a camera, getting heckled by my own waitress, but the capper of the evening was when Al Gilbert, the owner of the building, showed up. Al came over and asked to talk to me alone. I was still a little upset by Nina, so I didn't notice Al's demeanor until we went outside and I noticed that he looked a little peeved. *Oh no, another guy who didn't like the show. Great,* I thought.

"Hey, you had them packed in tonight," Al said, as he looked away. Al usually looked me in the eye when he talked to me. "How much were you charging at the door?" he asked.

"Nothing," I replied. "We let them in free but we charged them for their drinks. Why? Is there a problem?" I asked.

"Yeah, I guess you could say there is a big problem," Al said in his gangster voice.

Oh, here it comes, I thought, *the reason we got the club for nothing.* This wasn't Vancouver, where a friend would let us have a club for no rent until we got the business off the ground. This was L.A., home of the big scammers. And it turned out that Al was one of the biggest scammers around—now he was about to lay it on me. "You know it costs money to operate this club. And what you took in at the bar didn't cover expenses. So I'm going to have to take this club back from you boys."

I looked at Al and realized something. *Fuck it! Take this fucking club and shove it up your ass, Al. I don't want to be in business with a prick like you. You are a mean old thief who treats his own brother like shit. A mean, cheap, old fuck who steals equipment though he has the money to pay for it.* I thought these things, but I never expressed them. I just turned and walked out the door, feeling good about the show we just did and looking forward to the next one.

The next show was a week later, at the Troubadour on Santa Monica. Cheech and I showed up early and sat at the bar with the rest of the celebrities. Janis Joplin was there wearing a boa and looking like an old-time movie star. Cheech and I were still buzzed about our First Stage experience. We laughed at the sleazy way Al took the club back after we had done all that work. And we laughed at how stupid we were not to see what a con man Al was in the first place. He had us go down to the police station and get an operating license in my name—I guess because he didn't want any liability. Who the fuck knows what goes on in these people's heads? All we wanted was a place of our own where we could entertain, but I should have known that it is almost impossible to be both the entertainer and the club owner. One or the other suffers, and in my case it was the clubs that suffered and went under. I think Al saw that coming and pulled the plug before he suffered any more losses.

The emcee greeted Cheech and me warmly and asked if we were ready to go on. We nodded our heads and he went on-stage and gave us a long and detailed introduction. The stage at the Troubadour was built to accommodate folk singers, who sing very intimate and sometimes very soft and gentle songs, so the audience's attention has to be directed entirely at the stage. The atmosphere was almost churchlike, which made it perfect for Cheech and me—the club was a mini theater, perfect for our act.

That night was special because there were people in the audience who were giants in the industry, and they had come to see Cheech and Chong. We performed what was probably our best show that night. No one heckled and no one left offended . . . except for Frank Zappa. Frank had a reputation for being really off the wall when it came to Chicano humor. He was not Chicano, but he had adopted Chicano sensibilities and humor from spending time with the Chicano members of his band, the Mothers of Invention, from East L.A. However, according to our sources, Frank was not impressed with our act. He was so antidrug that our very first bit about the Chicano lowrider and the hippie was his worst nightmare. Frank was known to fire any of his band members if he found out they did drugs. Ironically, Frank was a chain smoker, drank copious amounts of coffee, and eventually died at an early age.

There was another heavy in the music business there that night—Lou Adler. We didn't meet him, but friends of Cheech's friends told us that Lou was laughing hard at our craziness.

"Who is Lou Adler?" I asked.

"He is a big record producer," Cheech explained. Cheech knew everyone who was anyone in Hollywood. I was amazed at his knowledge of the business. And I was even more amazed at his memory. Cheech could hear a song and know the lyrics after one listen. He has a photographic memory and he reads everything he gets his hands on. He was the brightest man I had ever met—that is, until we met Lou Adler.

"Well, let's call him up," I said.

Cheech called Lou the next day and he told us to meet him at his office in the A&M recording studio located on the corner of Sunset and La Brea in Hollywood. I picked Cheech up on the scooter and we scooted over to the meet. After we waited a few minutes in the reception area, his secretary, Cheryl, a very pretty dark-haired lady with a killer smile, escorted us into Lou's office. The office was decorated with gold albums from acts like The Mamas and The Papas, Jan and Dean, and Carole King. Carole King's song "Will You Love Me Tomorrow?" on her album *Tapestry*, was and still is my favorite recording of all time. The lyrics inspired me when I wrote "Does Your Mama Know About Me?" I loved her songs and I constantly listened to her album, which was at that time the biggest selling album of all time. As I looked at Lou's gold records, he sat in his chair looking at us and not saying a word. After a moment of silence he spoke. "So what can I do for you?"

Cheech and I looked at each other. We were not expecting

that question. We had assumed that Lou would be like the other would-be managers who told us what they could and could not do for us right away. This time it was different. He was asking us what we wanted.

"We want to do a comedy record," I replied. I had not discussed this idea with Cheech. In fact, we never even had a plan. But after looking at the gold records, my improvisational training took over and supplied me with the proper response.

"OK, so what do you need?" Lou asked again, not showing any emotion or excitement.

"A thousand dollars and a tape recorder," I replied. I didn't look at Cheech because this was pure improvisation.

"OK," Lou replied. He called for Cheryl and told her to cut a check for a thousand dollars.

"Uh, that's a thousand each," Cheech added.

Lou gave each of us a thousand-dollar check and told us to come in the next day to pick up the tape recorder, and that was the end of the first meeting. Cheech and I scooted home to give our ladies the good news. Man, we were flying high that day.

I gave Shelby the check and told her what happened. I was no longer allowed to handle our money, which was fine with me. I did not want to have that responsibility, but Shelby had studied accounting in school and was excellent with money. That day she walked down to the corner gas station and purchased a 1960 MGB sports car for seven hundred dollars.

Cheech and I showed up bright and early to pick up our tape recorder and begin rehearsing for the record. We found an empty little screening room on the A&M lot and began to rehearse. The A&M lot was the original movie studio where Charlie Chaplin filmed some of his famous comedies. And the screening room was where he watched these masterpieces, so the vibe was ripe with comedy energy.

We had brought our costumes to help us get into character, and the first piece was to be an encounter between a dope dealer and a hippie. Cheech donned a heavy wool overcoat and a felt hat and stepped outside to begin the bit. I was inside the air-conditioned room with the tape recorder running, waiting for him to knock on the door. The door locked automatically, so his knocking took me by surprise.

"Who is it?" I replied in my stoner voice.

"Open up, I got the stuff," Cheech replied in a whisper.

When I didn't answer, Cheech knocked again. The needle on the tape recorder moved with each knock so I knew we were getting it all on tape and I got into character. "Who is it?" I asked.

This time Cheech's voice was a little desperate and pissed off. "It's me, man, open the door. I think the cops saw me."

At this point I was laughing because Cheech was getting pissed off that I wouldn't open the fucking door. He knocked again only this time it was more of a banging.

"Who is it?" I answered again in the dumb stoner voice. I was laughing so hard inside I almost peed my pants.

"It's me, Dave! I got the stuff, now quit fucking around and open the door."

I was laughing so hard that I could hardly get the answer out. "Dave?"

"Yeah, Dave."

"Dave's not here!" When I said that line all hell broke loose.

"Come on, man, open the fucking door and quit fucking around. It's hot out here . . ."

On that line I opened the door and ducked out of the way as a red-faced Cheech came charging into the room. I thought he was going to hit me as he flung off the hat and coat.

"It's fucking hot out there man! I could have died from heat exhaustion." Cheech was suffering because it was probably more than one hundred degrees in the little courtyard. But as soon as I rewound the tape and we listened to the bit, he forgot all his discomfort.

We listened to the bit over and over for at least an hour before taking it up to Lou's office. Lou immediately booked time for us in the main A&M studio and we recorded the bit that night. Somehow Lou sent copies to radio stations across America, and the next morning we were awoken by phone calls from friends telling us to turn on the radio and listen to "Dave's Not Here."

Radio stations would play our bit every hour on the hour, and fans still wanted to hear it again and again. That bit became part of America's vocabulary. Guys named Dave were tortured with "Dave's not here" whenever they introduced themselves. Cheech and Chong had arrived in the hearts and minds of America, and we were on our way to becoming the biggest-selling comedy recording stars of all time.

CHAPTER ELEVEN

BLIND, BABY!
CAN YOU HEAR ME?

Los Angeles, California, 1971

After recording "Dave," we did our Blind Melon Chitlin' bit, in-spired by T-Bone Walker's 1969 performance in Vancouver. We improvised the entire bit in about three takes. Cheech played a hipster record producer who calls Blind, "Blind, baby." The year was 1971, at the very height of the music industry's popularity. Record albums and 45s were sold by the millions all over the world, making scores of record producers such as Phil Spector wealthy beyond their wildest imaginations. And with their wealth came corruption and greed. Dating back to the 1950s, DJs like Alan Freed put their own names on songs that were written by other people to collect record royalties to go with the graft they were already paid just for playing the record on their radio shows. Chuck Berry's hit "Maybellene" was one example. So Cheech's parody of a record producer in the studio with Blind Melon Chitlin' turned out to be a classic in many ways.

I would pretend to be blind and asleep, and Cheech would say, "Blind, baby, can you hear me? Blind, baby? ... Hey, he ain't deaf too, is he?"

"Uh, no, J. R., I think he's sleeping ..." [*Sounds of Blind snoring ...*]

"Well, wake him up. We are wasting time here! Blind, baby, can you hear me now?"

"Uh, yeah . . ." Blind answers in his deep, fucked-up drunk voice.

The "Uh, yeah" answer was inspired by Floyd Sneed. The original drummer for Three Dog Night, Floyd's humor was natural and very real. He used to imitate his uncle, who always answered the telephone with, "Uh, yeah," and often held his entire side of the conversation with those two words alone. Most, if not all, drummers have a wicked sense of humor because of their timing. Rhythm and timing are everything in music and comedy. Peter Sellers, the legendary comic, started his career as a jazz drummer.

When we came to the part when Blind finally starts singing, I improvised, "Going downtown gonna see my gal. Gonna sing her a song. Gonna show her my ding dong."

"Uh, cut! Blind, baby, we need you to enunciate . . . let's go over the lyrics . . . tell us, Blind, what exactly is a ding dong?"

We hear the sound of a zipper, indicating Blind's fly is opening, as the assistant says, "I think he's going to show you . . . !" The entire studio gasps at the size of Blind's ding dong, prompting the producer to shout, "We'll never get that on the album cover."

To my knowledge this was the first innuendo to get past the morality police. The bit received enormous radio play when the album was released all over America, Canada, and Australia. That was the genius of Lou Adler—and Cheech and Chong. We would record these gems and Lou would listen to them and give us feedback if he felt something was missing. Lou also scored music to some of the bits. But for the most part, he gave us the freedom to create our own little fantasy world in a little mix-down room at A&M records.

Lou had decided it would be better—and cheaper—to move us out of the studio and into one of those rooms because we worked out our ideas while we recorded them, which meant a lot of downtime for the engineers. The little mix-down room was the perfect atmosphere in which to create comedy without running up a large studio tab.

But Lou did more than just produce our records. He was one of the most eligible bachelors in Los Angeles, and he dated the most beautiful women on the planet. He was involved with Britt Ekland at the time we came into his life. Britt was his connection to the jet set, the rich playboys and playgirls of the world whose main occupation was going to parties. Britt and Lou were famous for their parties at his Bel Air home, where Cheech and I would hobnob with elite showbiz legends.

We were glassy-eyed with celebrity overload. There was someone famous everywhere you looked. I remember once trying to get past some guy who was holding court in the middle of the room. I finally pushed him aside, only to realize I had just touched Mick Jagger. Mick was so absorbed with the lady he was talking to that he didn't even look at me.

I had seen Mick in person before, in Vancouver, a few years before our gig at the Forum. The Stones were booked at the hippie club right above the Elegant Parlour, where Bobby Taylor and the Vancouvers were playing with a couple of members of James Brown's band. The place was filled to overflowing and we could not have fit another body in the club if we had to. The Stones had just finished playing to an empty club and were at the door, trying to squeeze in. My brother, Stan, was working the door and ignored Mick and Keith as only a doorman can ignore people. So the only thing they could do was to wave at us, hoping we would recognize them and get them in. I recognized them immediately, but there really was no room in the club, so I had to ignore them as well.

Here I was a few years later at a party with Mick himself. I wanted to say something to the legendary Stone, but this time he ignored me. I was at the party with Shelby, but I wanted to mingle, so we went our separate ways. Cheech was also there with his girl, but he too was on the loose, checking things out. I had the urge to smoke up, so I found a bedroom that I thought was uninhabited, only to find John Lennon sitting on the floor next to the bed. I had fired up a very stinky joint, so upon seeing John, I offered him a toke.

"Uh, no thank you," John replied. "I've got this immigration thing happening so . . . but thank you."

I looked at the Beatle and wanted to say something, but all I could do was puff on my joint, thinking, *This is John Lennon, the famous John Lennon, and he just refused a toke from me. How cool is that?* John was having women problems along with his immigration problems, so he was not in a talkative mood. He and Yoko Ono had broken up and he was now involved with a Chinese girl, May Pang. He was sitting on the floor mulling over his problems while I was busy staring at him like some idiot fan. But come on! This was the legend himself. John fucking-Strawberry-Fields-Forever, Imagine, Revolution, songwriting-genius Lennon! I had to stare. I couldn't help it. This man and his buddies changed the world with their songs, their movies, and their souls—all inspired by marijuana and LSD. Oh, yes, Lord.

Rod Stewart walked in, went to the mirror and started fussing with his hair, ignoring me and John completely. Rod fiddled with and pulled at his hair, seeming to fall even more in love with his reflection every second. I stood there paralyzed with celebrity overload. This was way too much for me. First Mick, then John, and now Rod.

"Uh, you want some of this?" I asked in my way-too-cool voice, as I offered him the joint.

"No, thank you! Got to take care of the voice," he said in his husky, trademark Rod Stewart voice.

I continued to puff on the joint that was way too stinky for the company I was in, and then slipped out to snuff out the roach in the bathroom. I took about five steps and came face-to-face with Jack Nicholson. I had just seen Jack in a movie the night before and now he was standing in the middle of the hallway trying to get past me.

I was really starstruck this time. No bullshit! He was the man! Jack "too fucking cool for his own good" Nicholson. When you see someone in person whom you just saw in a movie a few hours earlier, you feel like you know the guy personally. At least, that was the way I felt as I stood in Jack's way, staring at him as if he were a long-lost friend. Jack was not wearing his customary shades, probably because he was at his friend Lou Adler's home and figured he didn't need the dark glasses there. But I was an avid fan and I had Jack trapped without his sunglasses and looking a little . . . well, vulnerable.

"Jack, I saw *The Last Detail* and you were . . . wonderful," I blurted out.

Jack smiled that famous Jack Nicholson smile but did not respond. He made a halfhearted attempt to get past me, but I was the fan from hell, smiling at him, gushing over him. *Man*, I thought, *this is so fucking cool.* I tried to think of something intelligent to say because I really admired his acting. With his mannerisms and delivery, Jack can take you down roads in your mind you have never visited before, and sometimes leave you there. And he does it effortlessly. I could sense he wanted to end this conversation so I laid it on him.

"Jack, that scene where you stood in the mirror combing your hair over and over while you did the scene, was that in the script or did you improv that yourself? I mean, you have the thinnest hair and with the military haircut there was nothing to comb but there you are combing and combing . . . it was so cool, was all that written? Or did you just make it up?"

Jack just looked at me. He didn't say a word but just stared at me like I was showing him a turd, a fresh steaming turd. I felt myself disappearing, shrinking, drying up. He stared at me as if to say, *You fucking idiot! Is that all you can say? Is this why you stand in my way and ruin my high at a private party where we go just because we know pricks like you are not allowed in? Is this why you exist? To bug the hell out of us celebrities who just want to be left alone to drink, snort coke, and fuck adoring fans? Why don't you get out of my face and let me continue on my way forgetting that we ever met . . . OK?*

Jack never said a word. He looked at me for a full minute and proceeded to walk away. I stood there feeling ashamed and embarrassed. I had been dissed by my hero. I felt like smacking the shit out of him. My Canadian blood welled up in me and I started shaking. I was embarrassed, and now I was very pissed off. My pot high evaporated and I felt like I needed a shower.

I was very subdued the rest of the night. I remember meeting Carole King and one of her backup singers. They wanted to meet me because I had written "Does Your Mama Know About Me?" a favorite song of theirs. Carole and her friend had some nice things to say about the song that made me feel good. But I was still devastated by my encounter with Jack and I made a personal vow that night that I have kept to this day. I vowed that when I got as famous as Jack I would never disrespect my fans like that, no matter how stupid or obnoxious they were. I found out how much it hurts to be slammed and ignored by someone you idolize and admire; you never really recover from that kind of celebrity abuse. If you're famous and don't want to be bothered, then don't come out. Keep your ass home at your gated estate and be alone.

I have had occasion to be in Jack's presence since then. In fact, it was a ride to a Lakers game with Jack that inspired "Basketball Jones." Lou Adler and Jack have had Lakers front row seats for decades now and have attended almost every game since the team moved to L.A. One night Lou got tickets for Cheech and me and we were supposed to ride with him, but for some reason we ended up with Jack. We met at the Roxy and drove with Jack to the Forum. When we got close to the arena, the traffic was heavy, so instead of waiting in line with the rest of the basketball dorks, Jack pulled his big-ass Mercedes into the oncoming traffic and started speeding down the inside lane on the wrong side of the road. I froze as I saw my life flash before my eyes, watching the oncoming traffic swerve to get out of the way.

Right in the middle of this horror ride, Cheech began to sing. Whenever Cheech got nervous he would begin to sing. He would take a popular song and add his own crazy words to it. That night it happened to be a version of "Love Jones," a popular R & B song at the time, only he made up his own words and changed it to "Basketball Jones." "Basketball Jones, I got a basketball jones, I got a basketball jones, oh baby, woo woo woo." And for some reason the danger passed us by in that funny musical moment. We recorded the master the next night. This was the Cheech and Chong way—Cheech would do it, I would hear it and add lyrics, and Lou would polish it and add the music. We had a factory going for a while there.

We finished our first album and hit the road, starting in Rochester, New York, at Lee Grills's Pizza Parlor. Lee and his sons were into rock and roll, so they booked acts. People would be served fresh, hot pizza and be entertained all night, which was totally cool for musicians, but not so cool for comedians. It was difficult to keep people's attention while someone was screaming into a mike, "NUMBER 42 . . . NUMBER 42 . . . YER PIZZA IS READY!" Especially when they would yell right over the punch line! But you can't stop pizza.

Carly Simon was the other act on the shared bill. She was at the height of her fame and beauty. Carly Simon is a beautiful woman. One of America's top ten beauties of all time, in my opinion top five! And she can sing and write incredible songs. It was such a treat to be with her—we enjoyed that part of the gig immensely. The after party, however, was a different matter.

This was Cheech and Chong's first road trip, and we didn't know the rules. We sure did not know the number one rule of the road: Never party with the fans after the show. No matter what the temptation, ignore the bait. Don't get sucked in. Stay in your room. All of these lessons had to be learned the hard way. The reason you don't want to accept invitations to after parties is that you will be the main attraction. After finishing a grueling two-and-a-half-hour show, you arrive at the party, and guess who the entertainment is? Why it's you, of course. The one thing worse than being the entertainment is being totally ignored. So it is a lose-lose situation, no matter how you look at it.

The ride to the party was more entertaining than we expected. Lee Grills, the owner of the pizza joint, told his bouncer/doorman to "take care" of us. He was to drive us to the party and then make sure we got home safely. But this guy was a major nutcase, an ex–Vietnam combat soldier who probably to this day doesn't know how he survived the war. He was a point man during the fight at Hue, where the Viet Cong turned the fortunes of war against the Americans by mounting an all-out offensive, causing enormous loss of life on both sides. I'll call him Chuck because I am afraid to use his real name. Chuck was an all-star military man, from his haircut to the two automatic pistols he carried with him wherever he went. The pistols were fully loaded and ready to kill. Chuck had expected to die in Vietnam and the fact that he survived really bothered him. He told Cheech and me how bad he felt about living when his comrades in arms had perished in the war. He drove fast over the icy roads, barely glancing at the road as the tires slipped and slid around hairpin turns.

The car almost left the pavement more than a few times, and Cheech was singing nervously as we motored down the road. When we arrived at the party, I gave a silent thank-you to the unseen helpers who got us there alive.

As we walked into the house, we heard our album playing in the background. Every now and then people would stop to listen to the punch line, and then it was back to their conversations. I sat and studied the crowd. At one point a fan came up to me clutching a rare recording of Lightnin' Hopkins that he wanted to play for me. He gently placed the record on the turntable and placed the needle even more gently on the record. A scratchy song started emanating from the record player, causing the guy to sit cross-legged with his eyes closed, taking in the rare recording as if it were a religious ceremony and the singer was God. Old Lightnin' was wailing the blues something furious when suddenly the needle scratched across the rare record as someone snatched it up from the turntable and replaced it with a disco record. The record's owner rose out of his lotus position like a Samurai warrior ready to do battle while the record snatcher joined his buddies, who were laughing and drinking beer in the other room. The look on the record collector's face was one of classic horror. He was mortally wounded by the scratch on his prized possession. This was great material. I ended up using the bit on "Earache My Eye."

Our next memorable gig around that time was in Aspen, where we performed at a bar with the Flying Burrito Brothers, one of whom—Bernie Leadon—would soon help found the Eagles. The opening act was a one-armed bongo player who did a hell of a job. The audience liked the first show so much they all decided to stay for the second one. We were not used to performing back-to-back shows for the same audience, so we started writing like crazy, trying to piece together a second act. We pulled it off and after the gig we relaxed at the bar for a well-deserved party.

Cheech and Barbie were going through some hard times in their relationship. Barbie was the actress; she felt she was the one who was supposed to make it, and once it became apparent that Cheech was the star, things started to go bad. The more famous Cheech got, the more toxic their relationship became. They broke up in Aspen and our roadie Jimmy booked Barbie a ticket for home.

I remember that Aspen trip very well because it was when we took our last acid trip. The acid was some special "window pane" stuff that was going around the Denver area. We had a day off, so Shelby and I thought it would be a cool idea to drop the acid and take Precious to see *Thumbelina* at a movie theater out in the suburbs. We took a cab there and just as we walked into the theater and sat down, the acid suddenly came on very strong. Precious immediately became engrossed in the film, but I was having a hard time relaxing because kids were scurrying up and down the aisle like little rats. When I started watching the movie I was shocked to see it was a story about a young girl who is being forced to marry a rat. The acid started making things become too real and suddenly the little kids running around *were* rats! Against her will, the young woman on the screen was being forced to marry the biggest, most disgusting rat I had ever seen. I started freaking out and that, in turn, freaked out Shelby, who grabbed me and said, "I don't like this movie."

"I don't like this movie either," I whispered.

The entire theater was crawling with rats that scurried over the seats and under our feet. It was so frightening that we had to get out of there before we were eaten alive. I grabbed Precious, who protested all the way to the exit, "What? Where are we going? I want to watch the movie. It's not over yet."

I pushed open the exit door and we walked out into the cold. The door slammed shut behind us and as we looked around, we realized that we were outside in the cold with no plan for getting back to our hotel. The field behind the theater seemed to stretch for miles. We waded through the snow and found the front of the theater. It was closed up tight, so we started walking down the road in search of a service station where we could call a cab and get our acid-soaked minds back to the safety of our hotel.

The acid kept bringing on images of rats scurrying around my feet, and of the woman who was about to marry the big one. Shelby clung to me as we walked. She was going through her own rat torments. Precious tried to trundle through the snow, but it was too difficult for her little feet, so I picked her up and prayed for help. We finally came across a service station that was open and walked into the warm, grease-scented cashier's office.

"Hi, uh, we need a cab?" I spoke and watched the icy words

fall out of my mouth. The acid was peaking now. I saw images and I did not know whether they were real or fantasies. Shelby tried to talk, but she was also peaking and could only giggle. We were a complete mess.

The service station attendant finally showed us a telephone.

"Don't be too long. It's a business phone," he said looking at us with disgust.

"OK, thank you." Every time I spoke I could see the words and I could hear an echo. Shelby was giggling quite hard as she shook from the effects of the acid and the cold. Precious kept looking at each of us with a look in her eye that started to scare me.

I hope she doesn't tell the attendant how fucked up we are, I thought, very paranoid now. *Oh great, now I am paranoid for no reason. But wait, the attendant looks like a rat.* And he did. He had long teeth in front like a rat and he scurried around like a rat.

"Are you going to use the phone?" His voice boomed in my ear, causing me to whimper and jump nervously.

"Uh, yeah . . . We need a taxi?" I said, watching the words fall out of my mouth, in color no less.

"So call one," he answered in his loud, scary voice.

"I don't know the number," I answered, but it wasn't my voice. It was the voice of the acid. "Sir, we are from out of town and we don't know where we are, so would you please call a taxi for us?" The spirit inside me took over and started to make sense. Thank you, Jesus!

The attendant took the phone from my hand and dialed a number. "Hey, Jackie, we need a cab over to the gas station . . . just a minute . . . Hey, where are you going?"

Shelby and I huddled together as the acid kept peaking

stronger and stronger, leaving Precious as the only one who could effectively communicate with the outside world.

"We want to go home to our hotel, please," Precious said in a strong clear voice that tinkled like Christmas bells. The acid was now overwhelming and I started to get the giggles, so I looked away. When I looked back, I saw Precious hand the guy a room key with the name of the hotel on it. The guy relayed the message to the dispatcher and within a few minutes a cab pulled up and we were taken to the hotel.

And so ended our three-year love affair with LSD. It had changed our world and it had put me on a path to artistic and financial success, but it was over. The thrill was gone, but the effects lingered on for—well, I still get an acid flash every once in a while. The spiritual effects and the revelations never leave. They have never left me, anyway. The secrets that LSD revealed to me changed my life forever. And I know deep in my heart that the helpers or angels that are around us were the ones who directed me to that soul-expanding drug, and for that I will forever acknowledge them, wherever I am, in whatever I do. Thank you, Jesus.

Our career without acid continued to flourish under the guidance and management of Lou Adler. Cheech and I did an album a year for seven years. We won a Grammy for *Los Cochinos* and sold millions of records to fans around the world. A day doesn't go by without some fan telling me where they were and what they were doing when they first listened to one of our albums.

My older boy, Paris, wasn't born when we recorded them, but as soon as he was old enough he listened to them faithfully, and like so many skateboarders before him, he had his favorite bits. It was fun watching him grow up enough to understand just what was making his older friends laugh so hard. He understood the poop jokes, but the sexual innuendos stayed out of his reach until he became a teenager. The bit "T.W.A.T." always made him laugh, but he never knew why until his skateboarding buddies clued him in to the joke when he was thirteen. (T.W.A.T. was the official acronym for Tactical Women's Alert Team.) He never asked me, of course. And had he asked me, I doubt I would have told him. Knowledge about sex is acquired from older cousins, siblings, and friends, and rarely shared by parents. It was always the older cousins who you could rely on to make you hip to the finer things in life. At least that was the way it was for me and for Cheech. I had an older cousin who let my brother and me look at his collection of nudie magazines. You don't get that kind of firsthand knowledge in school. We had to rely on pool halls and bowling alleys, where some old perv would show us dirty pictures. And it would be years of frustration and sore balls before I was given the relief I had been seeking all my teenage years. It was years of kissing and fondling and secret masturbation before a girl finally took pity on my young eager-to-get-laid ass and gave me her twat.

Ah, the memory of that night will stay with me until the day I die. It was so sweet and brief. It occurred outside on a warm summer night—on the side of a hill, no less. I had barely gotten started when suddenly, I was finished! The girl barely had time to spread her legs when, after a couple of ecstatic thrusts, I blew my load and that was that! The relief was tremendous, not only for my poor balls, which had grown so used to swelling and turning blue, but for my self-esteem. That night I became a man. And as I lay there exhausted from two pelvic thrusts after years of waiting, I thought of a stupid joke, a Chinese proverb: "Man who make love on hill not on level." My partner in deflowering did not appreciate me laughing because she thought

I was laughing at her. In fact, she became quite pissed at my premature finish and told me in a not quite sweet voice to get the fuck off her. But nothing could erase my happiness. As I lay there on the hill with my pants down around my knees, looking up at the heavens, I said, "Thank you, Jesus . . ." and I meant it from the bottom of my balls.

CHAPTER TWELVE

OUR FIRST MANSION

Malibu, California, 1972

Cheech rented a house in the Hollywood Hills and became the party guy in town. Without Barbie he was a free man. While he dated a bevy of eligible Hollywood ladies, one in particular fed my admiration for the Cheech charm. Joni Mitchell, the genius Canadian songwriter, was entangled with Cheech for a while. Gaye Delorme, the guitarist, was staying with Cheech when Joni was over with David Geffen, who was Joni's personal manager at the time. Gaye was trying to convince Joni to buy a Canadian-built acoustic guitar, but David Geffen shot the deal down when he said he didn't especially like the guitar. David knew the music business and Joni respected his opinion, so she passed on the guitar. This did not stop the Canadian from trying. Gaye wrote the music and the riff for a tune soon to be known as "Earache My Eye" . . . or "Mama Talking to Me." Gaye came up with the music and the first line, "Mama talking to me," and I added, "trying to tell me how to live, but I don't listen to her cause my head is like a sieve . . . My daddy he disowned me cause I wear my sister's clothes. He caught me in the bathroom with a pair of panty hose."

I was the first to buy a house in Malibu. Shelby, Precious, and I were still living in the little apartment on La Jolla between Santa Monica and Melrose with our landlord friends Frank and

Rosie Bartolotti. It was a perfect setup for us because Frank and Rosie had become our L.A. family. They helped us in so many ways. Shelby and Precious would eat with them when I was on the road. Rosie taught Shelby how to be a wife Italian-style, which included whipping up a four-course Italian meal on a moment's notice. Up until then, I was the designated cook in our relationship. One time Shelby was visiting Rosie when I called up to tell her that supper was ready. Rosie looked at Shelby and asked, "Does Tommy do the cooking?" When Shelby answered in the affirmative, Rosie immediately took her aside and began teaching her how to cook Italian food. Shelby became a fabulous cook, and each time I sit down to one of her meals, I send a thank-you to Rosie.

Between recording albums and making personal appearances, Cheech and I began amassing enough wealth to buy our own homes. A friend turned me on to a realtor who showed me the house in Malibu. The owner and builder of the house was a gentle old cowboy by the name of Byron Vandergriff, who had designed and built quite a few homes in and around Los Angeles. Byron handpicked the land years before he bought it. He used to visit the spot when he was a boy, back when Malibu was still one huge ranch owned by a single family. I could picture the then-young cowboy fantasizing about the dream house he would build when he eventually owned the land. Byron's dream came true, and now he was passing his dream on to me. He was ready to scale his life down to an apartment in the city, where he and his beautiful wife, Margaret, would live out their years in comfort.

Byron's home on Bonsall Drive was his pride and joy. The square living room was copied from a home in Hawaii with twenty-foot brick walls and a wood-beamed roof that rose in the center like a tent designed to withstand high winds. The living room had space for three living-room settings and a dining-room table that could seat twelve people. The table was also a Vandergriff design and part of the many pieces left to us when we purchased the home. It was actually an estate, since the house was situated on close to three acres and included a riding ring and a separate garage/guest house/maid's quarters on the property. The landscape included woods of forty-foot fir trees, a gentleman's garden that took up an acre, complete with a tractor, a long driveway, a parking area for ten vehicles, and three dogs. The dogs were left along with the furniture because it was a dog's paradise. Hey, it was *my* paradise. The entire estate was for sale for six hundred and fifty thousand dollars! This was 1973, and Malibu had not caught on like it has today.

When we purchased the Bonsall house we had no idea what we were doing. We went from not being able to afford an eighty-five-dollar-a-month rental unit to owning a seven-thousand-square-foot home on three acres, with a four-car garage and a separate guest house. It was overwhelming at first, but rewarding. A dream come true. The American rags-to-riches success story.

Byron gave me daily lessons on how to run the estate. He showed me how to drive the tractor he used to plow the gardens. He told me the names and histories of the various exotic plants, fruit trees, and shrubs that grew in abundance on the property. And he told me how to treat the help, the Mexican family who ran the estate when Byron was away. The father was the caretaker and gardener, and he also worked on other properties in the area. His daughter, Sofia, did the domestic chores, so the family lived in the maid's quarters. Little did we know what was in store for us; the family eventually extended to their brothers, cousins, and friends. This was our very first home and we were starry-eyed. Shelby and I loved the challenge of this beautiful property that was all ours.

Cheech immediately started looking for his dream home and soon found a little beach house that Katharine Ross and her man, Sam Elliot, the famous cowboy actor, had been renting for a couple of years. They loved the place, but it was put on the market and Cheech swooped in and bought it. A wood-framed bungalow used at one time by fishermen, the house had been moved to the bluff overlooking the Pacific Ocean from another location. Cheech bought his dream house for around two hundred thousand dollars and recently put it up for sale for six million! Oh, man, if we had known then what we know now.

Cheech hired Robert Gilbert, a friend of his from school, to give it the Cheech touch. Robert Gilbert was a renowned artist, sculptor, and builder, who designed and built a house for Bob Dylan down the beach from Cheech. It was around this time that Cheech met a very beautiful waitress who worked at the Roxy, a nightclub owned by Lou Adler and a favorite hangout for rock stars. We featured the Roxy in *Up in Smoke* as the club where the battle of the bands took place, and where the van made of marijuana finally burned to the ground. Cheech was a regular at the Roxy and his waitress girlfriend Rikki soon became the first Mrs. Marin. She moved into the newly remodeled beach house, where she pursued her love of horses and gardening, and worked on her acting career. She was in *Cheech and Chong's Next Movie* as the rich daughter of Edie McClurg, she was one of the Fifis in *Things Are Tough All Over*, and one of the princesses in *The Corsican Brothers*.

Rikki and Shelby soon became best friends and life at that time was beyond good. Life was perfect.

Precious also found a friend her own age right next door when she went exploring and found an opening in the forty-foot laurel hedges that surrounded the estate. When she went through the opening like Alice in Wonderland, she found a little blonde-haired girl her own age on the other side of the hedge. It was too perfect. The Malibu years were filled with orchards, long country roads, horses, three young, healthy daughters, and one bouncing baby boy. We named him Paris after our favorite city. Precious, Robbi, and Rae Dawn were the big sisters to our fat, little, cuddly, blond, blue-eyed boy.

Rae Dawn was accepted into Ojai Valley School, immediately found the hippest people to hang with, and blossomed in the laid-back hippie atmosphere. I sent for my mother and father and fixed them up in the guest room at Bonsall. My dad drove Rae Dawn, Precious, and Robbi whenever they needed to be taken somewhere. Pop loved his job because he loved to drive, and that was a good thing because when you lived in Malibu, you had to drive everywhere. The corner store was a good mile and a half from the house. Mom loved the tranquil atmosphere of the Bonsall house and would sit for hours in the garden enjoying the Malibu weather. Years of living in Canada and enduring long, harsh winters made their extended holiday that much nicer.

Precious attended a little country schoolhouse where kids were taught skills like, "When you see a rattlesnake on the road, take ten steps backward away from the snake then turn and run as fast as you can." Shelby started taking horse-riding lessons and I purchased a couple of horses from Cheryl, Lou's secretary, for Robbi and Precious. Robbi was totally into the horse thing and would stay out at Cheryl's place on weekends, riding and grooming their horses.

Cheech and I enjoyed the Malibu life as only two stoners

could. Our common addiction at the time was playing basketball. We had a basketball jones and we played every chance we got. We found the pickup basketball scene in every city where we toured, we played at the Hollywood YMCA with actors and musicians, and we played a number of charity games with Marvin Gaye and the Jackson Five (minus Michael).

I had a hoop put up over the garage and we had many a fun game of 21 on that court. We even played a game with Bob Dylan. Talk about legends! Bob Dylan wrote and recorded so many meaningful, historic songs that epitomized the soul of America, righteous and strong. Bob had a good jump shot and some pretty good moves, but when he tried driving past me for a lay-up, the Canadian ice-hockey player in me came out and I dumped him on his ass with a ticky-tack foul. "Ticky tack" is a term used excessively by the late, great Lakers announcer Chick Hearn. It means the foul was not extreme and the play could have resumed, but the ref called it anyway, making the foul ticky tack.

The key to basketball is passing at the right time—then no one is going to beat you, not if you are playing like a team. I pointed that out to Charles Barkley one night when I was sitting courtside at a Clippers game. Sir Charles did not take kindly to my advice and threatened the guy sitting next to me because he thought he was the one heckling him. Charles made some very crude suggestions about the man's wife.

Heckling when you are sitting courtside is an art that must be learned. You must never use volume. You are courtside and players have good hearing, so you can whisper and they will hear you. In fact, they will hear a whisper long before they pay attention to someone yelling. They hear the yells, but they are ready for yells. Somehow, using a normal speaking voice allows them to hear every word clearly. I kept a running dialogue going whenever Charles was in hearing range. "Barkley is such a ball hog. Look, he never passes the ball when he should. Watch him . . . See, what a ball hog!" I could see I was getting to him, and before long Sir Charles blew his cool. He went on and on about what he was going to do to that innocent man's wife. The officials, who were a distance away and couldn't hear the dialogue, thought he was just chatting it up with a fan. I acted like I was shocked at the guy myself, pretending to be surprised.

On the next play, Sir Charles drove past the entire Clippers team and finished with a resounding dunk that had everyone running for cover. My remarks had wakened the sleeping giant. Charles turned into a basketball-playing demon, intercepting passes, throwing down threes, driving, and dunking. I smiled, knowing I had gotten to the big guy just by letting him overhear my critique of his game.

In addition to being addicted to basketball, Cheech and I were also learning tai chi from a former college basketball player named Joel Lasker. Joel would teach us on the lawn at my house, going over the moves until we all got them down, or at least appeared like we understood him. Cheech became quite good at tai chi and included it in his daily routine, which centered around meditation. He still practiced the meditation techniques of the Maharishi Mahesh Yogi and would literally spend hours in meditation before he started his day, sometimes ending his day with another hour. I wasn't into meditation at the time. I was led to believe you had to perform some special rites and when I was told about the effects of meditation I thought to myself, *I'll just stick to my pot, thank you.* But I do attribute much of our success as a comedy duo to Cheech's discipline in practicing meditation.

Shelby and I threw quite a few parties at the Bonsall house. I remember my daughter Precious's sixth birthday party in particular. I was at the Trancas market getting stuff for the party when I ran into Martin Sheen. He had just moved to Malibu and was relatively unknown to the community. I knew who he was because I was a big fan of his early movie, *Badlands*, directed by Terrence Malick. I had seen it at least a dozen times and was ready to see it a dozen times more. I loved everything about it, especially Martin Sheen's performance. He played a young, deranged killer opposite Sissy Spacek, who played his fifteen-year-old girlfriend. The dark, compelling love story between the two of them made a lasting impression on me. The movie was playing in a theater near Paul's Mall, a club in Boston where Cheech and I had just performed. I would duck out of the club between shows and watch the movie over and over until I could recite the dialogue line for line. So when I saw Martin at the market I immediately told him how much I loved the movie and I invited him and his boys Charlie and Emilio to my daughter's birthday party. Martin knew who I was and was very honored that I knew his movie and liked his performance. They showed up at the party and completely enjoyed the Malibu welcome.

The Bonsall house was perfect for having parties. The biggest drawback was that Shelby and I were too busy hosting to really enjoy them. Still, we met some very famous people at them—Anjelica Huston, Rene Russo, and Art Garfunkel, who commented to Lou as they pulled in the long driveway, "Damn! How many records do these guys sell?" Lou just smiled and said, "Enough to afford all this."

Kareem Abdul-Jabbar was also a frequent guest at my house and at Cheech's, where he would stay on the occasional weekend. Cheech looked like a member of the Lollipop Guild next to the 7'4" Kareem. Kareem was the best basketball player in the league, and he played well past his prime. He credits his longevity in basketball to his use of the magical herb that he shared with me on occasion.

Peter Sellers came out to the Malibu house, too. I played him a videotape of a couple of street performers doing mime on a San Francisco street. They were known as Shields and Yarnell, a husband-wife team who went on to star in their own television show, and their act involved following unsuspecting people around and miming their walk. Peter loved the tape, and clapped his hands and laughed like the little boy he was.

Peter loved crazy comedy and he fell in love with Cheech and Chong right from the beginning. Being a great jazz drummer, he appreciated our hip comedy in a way that only another musician could. He got all the humor and the little asides that we would insert just for musicians. And when Peter liked someone or something he became obsessive to the point of insanity. We loved Peter, though you never really knew which "Peter" you were going to be dealing with from day to day. He had enormous popularity and connections in England during his reign as the U.K.'s funniest actor, and he even had us do a tour there just so he could see our show and hang out with us.

When Cheech, Barbie, Shelby, and I arrived at Heathrow Airport, we were met by high-ranking immigration officials who gave us the VIP treatment and hustled us through a special checkpoint. This was before the fear of terrorism, so we never had to go through scanners or get felt up. We just had to follow the lady in the uniform and within minutes of disembarking we found ourselves in a courtyard where a long white limo was parked. As we approached the car, the rear window rolled down and a hand offered a huge chunk of hash as a welcoming gesture. The corner of the hash was burning and the smell of the kif filled the entire immigration area with a sweet, pungent, India-Pakistan hippie smell. When I close my eyes I can remember the smell and the warm happy feeling that came with it.

Peter then had the driver take us to his flat, located in a very nice upper-class section of London. When we arrived at his apartment, we were greeted by empty rooms. No furniture to speak of. No sofa, no chairs. No nothing! The place was empty. It had wall-to-wall carpeting and that was it. Peter, feeling the effects of the huge hash bar, kept walking into the walls. He would attempt to walk through a doorway and bump into the frame of the door. It was like watching Inspector Jacques Clouseau from the *Pink Panther* series.

Peter was a believer in the ancient Chinese art of feng shui, which involves directing the flow of energy in one's home or business with mirrors and wind chimes to amplify the positive and neutralize the negative. Feng shui masters use a compass to find the direction of the North Pole so the house or business can be brought into alignment with the stars. Ever the perfectionist, Peter was constantly moving furniture around, or in this case, not buying furniture at all. His weirdness translated into big money at the box office and his movies were the top-grossing comedies of all time—everyone had to sit back and watch the genius do his thing.

I had a special bond with Peter because we were both musicians-turned-comedians and could communicate on different levels, especially after smoking a ton of hash. The hash would bring one inside oneself, where the Kingdom is. This is the Paradise that Moses was looking for. The stillness that makes everything perfect. Inside is where It resides. Peter lived inside and showed the world the effects of his bond with the muse in his performances. And in the end, Peter and the muse became one.

In the movie *Being There*, Peter played a gardener who is

slightly retarded or "touched by God," as the native people would say. Peter's character, Chauncey Gardener, ends up becoming an adviser to the president of the United States because he is so honest and clear that his naive advice about gardening is mistaken for wisdom on how to solve the country's problems. And at the end of the movie Chauncey actually walks on water because he is pure. The film captured the real Peter Sellers and we were blessed when he became our biggest fan.

Later that week, Cheech and I performed at Ronnie Scott's Jazz Club with Blossom Dearie and the Jazz Messengers. The club featured the best jazz in the city and very little comedy, if any, but Peter made some calls and there we were in between sets by two jazz greats, performing our East Los Angeles humor. Peter was very wasted and spent most of the show with his head on the table passed out. We struggled with the show and the jazz audience, who did not come to see two young comedians do bits about smoking dope. When comedy does not work—that is, when a joke does not get laughs—the show takes on a whole different feeling. Moments like that make you realize that both the audience and the performers must be in sync for a show to work. There has to be a rhythm, a pulse that you can groove to for the act to work. If those elements are missing, the act suffers. No laughs = no fun and a long night.

Another curse for a comedian is getting up after a musical act. This is deadly because the people are there to hear music, not someone talking. Still, the gig was not exactly a disaster—as soon as we went into Blind Melon Chitlin', a music number, the place, and Peter, woke up. Peter was laughing hard, but as soon as we went into our big finish, the butt-sniffing dogs bit, we lost them. We were scheduled to do two shows that night, but right after we finished the first show, Ronnie Scott himself waked into the dressing room and offered us fifty quid and said, "Good show, mates, but here is fifty quid. Don't do the doggie bit, all right lads?"

We toured the rest of England from Manchester to Liverpool, playing at different venues along the way, mostly music clubs, but occasionally the promoter would throw a curve at us in the form of an all-girls private school. We were barely into our show in the school auditorium when the entire audience stood up and quietly exited the room row by row while we were still onstage! I kept saying, "Wait, don't go. You haven't seen the part where I fuck Cheech in the ass!" Sometimes the funniest part of a show is when it falls apart and you try to fix it by being even more gross. Hey, what else can you do? All you have to throw at them are words.

The rest of the shows were pretty good on the whole, considering we were doing East Los Angeles Chicano humor in England and managing to win them over. We learned a lot on that trip and enjoyed the experience of being in a small country that had produced so many giants. I have always felt that the United Kingdom is the white people's Africa. This is the motherland for talented English-speaking white people in all fields of the arts.

In September 1973, we toured Australia, hitting all the big cities, like Sydney, Melbourne, and Adelaide. The gigs were held at the local town halls and were packed with dope-smoking Aussies who loved our stoner humor. Actually, they loved us so much that the opening acts had a very hard time just getting through their sets. One band pissed the audience off so much that they started throwing beer cans at them onstage. It was unreal because no one even tried to stop them. I even saw a cop throw a beer can at the band from backstage. It was surreal. Like a movie. I was a little worried, but as soon as we hit the stage the audience settled down and enjoyed our show.

We did a bit that was originally performed by the Committee in San Francisco in 1965. We expanded into "The Old Man in the Park" and it was an Aussie favorite. This is the bit where I dress in a long overcoat and walk hunched over like an old man. After wobbling onto the stage I pretend that I am feeding birds in a park. I entice a bird with food and just when it gets within striking range, I smack it with my cane and mime putting it in a bag and setting it beside me. In the meantime, Cheech, dressed like a badass biker, appears on the scene and proceeds to stand in front of me and comb his hair. This causes me to react by spitting directly on his boot. Cheech stops combing and looks at his boot. Then he looks at me.

"Did you just spit on me, old man?"

"Ah, fuck off," I answer in my old man voice.

Cheech then walks behind me, leans over, and says, "Fuck off? You telling me to fuck off, man?"

I sit and glower at the young punk. Cheech stares at me with his mean biker stare, then begins to walk away.

"Yeah, run away, you goddamn, yellow, chickenshit bastard."

This stops Cheech in his tracks. He slowly turns and walks back as he says, "You got a dirty mouth, old man. You gotta watch who you talk shit to, man. You could be fucking with a serial killer." Cheech grabs my hat and starts steering me like a car, jamming the hat over my eyes as he yells, "We driving in the Grand Prix and Mario Andretti moves into first place. *Varroomm!*

"You let go of me you. You . . . goddamn monkey!"

"Huhuhu," he makes monkey sounds as he fucks with my hat.

"You know, you should have more respect for me. I could be your father!"

Cheech stops what he is doing and says, "What do you mean, you could be my father?"

"I used to fuck buffalos. And you look just like your mama!"

"Hey, don't you be talkin' about my mama now."

The old man takes a swat at Cheech's leg with his cane and the fight is on. Just when it looks like the fight is all fun and games the old guy clutches his heart and collapses on the stage.

"Come on, old man. You ain't hurt!" Cheech jumps around a little waiting for the old guy, who lays there motionless, to get up.

"Hey, old man, what are you doing? Hey, I never touched you, man! You started it! Come on, man, get up. Don't be dead, OK? Look, I'm not a real biker! Man? . . . Please don't be dead . . . I'm on probation, man. Oh geez! Man, they will send me back to the joint! Man, I don't want go back, man! Oh, please, God, don't do this to me . . ."

At this point the old man jumps up and says, "Scared the shit out of you, didn't I!" And blackout.

The Australian fans were different in every city. The Melbourne crowd seemed to be more stylish in their dress and in their ways, while the Adelaide crowd seemed to be transplants from San Francisco. We attended a party and met a guy who had been living in a briar patch, eating mushrooms that grew in cow shit, and tripping his brains out. The term "shit for brains" accurately described this weird young hippie with a taste for the 'shrooms. His hair was matted and his clothes were disheveled, and he had a glow in his eyes that could have been from the mushrooms or from hunger. He was also puffing on a series of Australian spliffs, offering us a hit whenever he paused in his rambling. It was like listening to a John Coltrane solo. He would start a story and then drift off into a different world, then he would stare at us intently, waiting for answers to a series of unasked questions.

Cheech used our time in Australia to hunt for art objects that were impossible to find in the United States. His cultured side had him searching the antiques shops for special jewelry and Tiffany and Lalique glass. He spent a small fortune amassing his collection, stuffing his little beach house with lamps and furniture and jewelry. He purchased a beautiful opal necklace for Rikki that dazzled the eye with its beauty, prompting comments from Shelby that made me realize Cheech was in a different league than I was when it came to giving great gifts. Shelby would prefer picking out her own gifts to trusting my taste.

Rikki and Shelby did not enjoy Australia as much as Cheech and I did because it was still a "man's country," where women were treated much like second-class citizens. This did not go over well with the two of them, who were used to getting special treatment because of their beauty and dynamite bodies. The girls would ask an Australian man a question, only to have the guy ignore them and answer directly to Cheech and me. This happened enough times that whenever we went there, the girls would leave the tour early and meet up with us in Fiji or Hawaii.

One time, Shelby took off for Hawaii with our new son, Paris, with plans to meet me when our tour was over. Cheech and I played the remainder of the tour and met an incredible blues singer named Renée Geyer, who electrified the audiences with her great voice and stage presence and held them spellbound with her talent. When the tour was finally over, I flew to Hawaii to meet Shelby and the baby. As we landed in Hawaii,

I realized that I had no clue where I was to meet Shelby. I had no idea which hotel they were at or even what area of Hawaii they were in. This was the era before cell phones, and we had no local friend or office where we could check in for messages. We were totally disconnected.

I tried to keep from freaking out as the reality of my situation became clear. I calmed myself by asking the Creator for help. This was the silent technique I learned before Cheech and I became successful: to leave everything in the hands of the Creator. The Helpers, as the *I Ching: The Book of Changes* would say. Let go and let God. What else could I do?

When the plane landed, I gathered my bags at baggage claim and got into a cab. When the cabbie asked the obligatory, "Where to?" I answered, "Uh, let's try the beach." To which the cabbie replied, "Which beach?"

"I don't know, so how about the most popular beach."

The cabbie turned and looked at me to see if I was drunk or something, then he said something under his breath about "howlies" and announced that the most popular beach in the world is Waikiki beach, where surfing was first invented. I felt very relaxed on the ride to the beach, enjoying the Hawaiian scenery as we drove. I felt the calmness of the Spirit come over me as we neared our destination. The driver pulled into the parking lot and collected his fare as I got my one suitcase.

"Good luck and enjoy Hawaii." The driver smiled in appreciation as he pocketed his big tip and drove away.

I turned and surveyed the pristine golden sand of the beach. *This really is the home of the gods,* I thought to myself as I walked, propelled by an unseen force. I saw the baby first. Little Paris sitting in the sand waving a little plastic shovel, dumping sand onto his chunky little legs. Then I saw Shelby lying on a towel, reading a softcover book.

"Hi, how was the trip?" she asked me casually, shielding her eyes from the sun as she looked up at me.

"Uh, fine," I answered. I took off my shirt and shoes and sat down beside her. "Where are we staying?" I asked casually. I was completely blown away by the ease with which I found her and Paris. I wanted to see if she was aware that I had no idea where she was going to be or where I could get in touch with her in case of an emergency. But she did not seem the least bit impressed with the fact that I found her on the beach among thousands of people and hundreds of beaches. "You know, I had no idea where to look for you guys," I said, trying to sound concerned.

Shelby ignored me as she dealt with the baby, who was now dumping sand on some other little guy. "Honey, don't throw the sand on the baby, OK? Dump it on yourself but not on the baby." Shelby gently took the shovel from Paris and started covering his legs with sand.

"I knew you would find us," she said. "You always do."

Hawaii was a special place for Cheech and Chong. First of all, I am half-Chinese and Cheech is Mexican, so we look vaguely Hawaiian. But it is our pot connection that makes us honorary citizens. Our records were a big hit in Hawaii because of ethnic and pot humor. The Hawaiian bud was legal for years until the Republicans and Richard Nixon started the DEA and began a worldwide persecution of pot smokers. But during the golden era of pot freedom, Hawaii had the best. Maui Wowie and Kona Gold were da kind that gave the Hawaiians their freedom of expression that usually took the form, "Hey, mon, give me another toke!"

Cheech and I played at the Hawaii Bowl more than a few times and sold out the venue every time. I guess our New Year's Day performance was the most notable. The concert was held in the crater at Diamond Head on the island of Oahu. I believe Sly and the Family Stone was the headliner, and the place was packed with both tourists and locals. I don't remember a whole lot of the concert itself because I had smoked up a little too much and was laid out in the tall elephant grass near the stage. I could not get up. So I just lay there staring at the clouds and listening to the concert. I heard the PA announce that they were looking for me, so I attempted to rise. But the harder I tried, the stronger the gravitational pull of the earth, so I just lay there until one of the frantic promoters found me. I know that Cheech and I performed, but I'll be damned if I can remember even the intro for that gig.

We were such hippies that as soon as we checked into the four-star hotel on the golf course, we immediately started looking for a hotel in town near the "people." Cheech and Rikki loved the hotel and did not want to move, but I insisted because the place was "too square, man." We did not belong there and the other guests did not want us there. Cheech was even mistaken for a hotel employee right when we checked in. He was sitting with the luggage, waiting to be taken to his room, when another guest gave him keys and told him to bring his luggage to his room while he went to the bar. We laughed at the possibilities of what we could have done with the guy's luggage had Cheech gone along with the assumption that he was the bellhop. I put a version of that event in *Next Movie*—a guy hands Red (Cheech's cousin) keys to his Ferrari and tells him to take care of it. Of course, Red thinks it's a present and drives away on an adventure.

We ended up taking a tab of acid and moving from the four-star hotel to a local rooming-house hotel that was one star away from being a ghetto. Cheech, buzzed on acid, kept asking, "Why did we move here?"

"The other place sucked, man. They treated you like a bell-hop. They don't like us, man! I don't want to stay at a place where people treat us like hippies."

"But we are hippies, man. And that hotel had twenty-four-hour room service!" This one doesn't even have toilets in the rooms."

That was true. The toilets were at the end of the hall. But we were buzzed on acid and we were "down with the people, man." I believe we eventually moved back to the hotel on the golf course, but not before spending the entire acid trip in the slum hotel.

We also played a show in Lahaina. The highlight of that gig was when Cheech and Rikki went on a weed run to the other side of the island to a place called Hana. Cheech had met the grower and was determined to buy the pot directly from the source, which meant chartering a small aircraft to fly them to the other side of the island. Rikki wanted to go to Hana to climb the mountain and explore the crater.

They took off early in the morning so they could accomplish all their goals and be back in time for the show. The weather was sunny and clear over on the Lahaina side of the island, but cloudly and cold on the Hana side. Cheech and Rikki landed at a small landing strip and rented a vehicle to take them to the bottom of the mountain, where they hiked halfway up and met with the grower, from whom they purchased an ounce of weed. They then proceeded to hike the rest of the way up the mountain to view the crater, and then hiked back down to their waiting aircraft.

In the meantime, I rose from bed around noon and strolled down to the health food store to buy a little breakfast. The owner of the store was sorting out dime bags of weed when I walked in. He noticed me staring at the weed and asked if I would like a bag. I immediately nodded a big yes and before I could say anything, he threw a bag of weed at me. I caught it and became intoxicated immediately by the smell of fresh-picked buds. I hurried home with my treasure and proceeded to do some heavy drug testing for the rest of the afternoon.

Cheech and Rikki showed up a few hours before showtime all tanned and exhausted from their ordeal. Cheech had a few scratches and bruises from his hike up the mountain, but he was glad that he made the trip and proudly showed me his trophy. He told me how he had to climb a fucking mountain and pay top price for the weed, but, "Check it out, man."

I paused to savor the moment. Then I showed him my bag, which was identical to his, except mine had more weed in it.

"Where did you get that?" he asked, as he compared the bags of smoke.

"At the health food store," I replied with a shit-eating grin on my face. I was stoned, and hearing his story made me want to scream with joy. Not because I was gloating or anything. Well, maybe a little. But the main reason I was so happy was because we had another bit to add to our memory bank. This was how Cheech and Chong made funny movies. Cheech would do the craziest things, then he would tell me about them and I would write them into the movies. We were like the tortoise and the hare. He was super quick and I was super slow. The perfect match.

We did the show at Lahaina at Shep Gordon's restaurant and again kicked some Hawaiian ass. The bit of the night was one about hitchhiking in Hawaii. Apparently, it was and prob-ably still is illegal to hitchhike in Hawaii. You have to hitchhike Hawaiian-style, where you just look like you need a ride. You don't stick out a thumb or make any sign that you need one. You stand still and make it look like you need a ride. This piece of information cracked me up and I did a rap about standing on the side of the road when a couple of Hawaiian dudes stopped their car and told me to get in. I got in and rode with them for a while until one of them asked me where I was going. When I told them the name of the hotel they said, "That's where we picked you up. You didn't need a ride."

"No."

"Then why did you get in the car?"

"Because you told me to," I replied.

They mumbled something about stoned hippies and drove me back to where they picked me up. "Next time don't look like you need a ride, OK, howlie?"

Our live act was getting better and better as the years and records rolled by. We found ourselves having to record between gigs, and sometimes even during gigs. The Quiet Knight in Chicago was a club where we would record while we worked. *Let's Make a Dope Deal* was recorded live at the Quiet Knight.

We always played Chicago during the winter, and it would be so fucking cold you could never really get warm.

Cheech and I were dabbling in cocaine at that time, and even though I would get deathly ill with a pneumonia-like sickness, we kept on accepting snorts of the deadly drug whenever they were offered. The only thing I could do was drink gallons of hot water with fresh lemons and stay in bed whenever possible. Somehow cocaine opens you up for all the bad bacteria that is floating around, especially when you snort it directly into your nose, which is right next to the brain. And the numbing effects of the coke enable you to snort far more than you normally would if you had any feeling in your nose.

Cheech and I were very lucky because our act really sucked when we were high on coke. That was a good thing. Can you imagine where we would have been had coke helped the act? And coke did help many comics with their act, giving them energy, insight, and a tremendously expensive coke habit. I had to give it up because of my health, and I am sure Cheech gave it up for the same reason.

One of the problems with street coke is that you never know what it is, exactly, you are exposing your brain to. The dealers cut the pure cocaine with agents like baby laxatives and other stuff, so the user never really knows for sure just what she is snorting. And once you are addicted to coke, say bye-bye to wife, kids, and job.

I talked to a holistic healer, and she told me that the reason people become addicted to drugs like coke and heroin is that it elevates the dopamine in your system, in much the same way as sex and thrill sports, such as sky diving. This is where marijuana differs from other drugs. Pot actually lowers the dopamine in one's system. You hear that, DEA? It lowers the dopamine, which explains why stoners become lazy and unmotivated. This also explains why one can quit pot without the unpleasant side effects associated with coke and smack. And this also explains why comics, artists, writers, and athletes prefer pot over hard drugs: because the user is in control of his habit.

Pot fueled Cheech and Chong during our heyday. Pot and to some extent, acid. The downside to pot is that it can cause depression because of the lower dopamine levels. But I somehow lucked out with my addiction to weightlifting. This is an activity that raises the dopamine levels in a healthy manner. A good, hard, sweaty workout is equivalent to a snout full of coke any day. Physical activity has saved my butt my entire life. And I am eternally grateful to my mentors in Vancouver, who made me quit smoking cigarettes and made me work out hard in the gym. They insisted I eat healthy and get lots of sunshine and fresh air. They also steered me toward California and Muscle Beach, where the real bodybuilders hung out, and where I would lie in the sun programming images of success into my being by "seeing myself successful."

CHAPTER THIRTEEN

WE'VE GOT TO
BE IN PICTURES

Malibu, California, 1977

So we started talking about movies.

We had turned down a television offer that was pretty sweet. Brandon Tartikoff, the president of NBC, offered us the show himself, but we turned it down. Actually, I turned it down. I think Cheech would have loved to have done the show, especially had he known how easy it is to do a television show compared with doing a movie. But I was the go-to guy and I knew that doing television can deal a death blow to an acting career. The television guys were hard to shake. They even sent a writer/producer on the road with us for three months to try to convince us to do the show. James Komax was the writer and actor on a hit sitcom called *The Courtship of Eddie's Father* and he loved Cheech and Chong so much that after we turned down the offer, he used the pilot he wrote for us and did the show with a New York comic named Freddie Prinze. The show *Chico and the Man* was from a bit Cheech and I did called "The Old Man in the Park" and from our record bit called "Pedro and Man." James combined these two bits into his show. I talked to him after the show came out, and he acknowledged he took our bits; but then I laughed and told him we got the bits from the

Committee and Second City so it was an even swap. No harm, no foul.

The *Chico and the Man* series with Freddie Prinze was an instant hit and played at the top of the charts for many years; however, in a tragic turn, Freddie took his life. His suicide really added to my fears about the pressure of working television so we stayed away from it.

Cheech and I were tired of the road for obvious reasons. We started repeating club and theater appearances, which forced us to constantly update the show and was a good thing. But it was the contant travel and living out of suitcases that got us down, especially knowing we both had beautiful homes we weren't enjoying.

We started urging Lou to get us a movie deal. I wrote a screenplay with Joel Lasker called *Jack and the Weedstalk*. It was my first attempt at being a screenwriter, and I really enjoyed it. It's soothing and fulfilling, especially when you are writing a script that no one will ever see. Without pressure, you can make the characters do whatever you want them to do. You can change whatever you want and make improvements wherever you feel like it. No one but you has the power to change a word or comma. No one. Naturally, when you write for producers who have strong opinions, writing can become a colossal headache. *Jack and the Weedstalk* was never submitted to Lou *or* Cheech.

While Lou was busy networking along the Malibu Beach and pitching Cheech and Chong to a major Paramount suit who had a house near his, we were out on the road working our usual venues and landing a nice monthly gig in Vegas. We scored a million-dollar deal to do a gig at the Aladdin Showroom three days a month for a year. The shows were at two in the morning so the regular dealers and casino workers would be able to catch our show. As sweet as the gig sounds, we earned every cent of that million. The two AM showtime was brutal! Las Vegas is the toughest place on the planet to go to bed early. It keeps you up all night with its ambience and hypnotic sounds, designed to keep the adrenaline flowing so you can stay up gambling.

Everyone gambles in Vegas. And everyone loses. Eventually. If you gamble there is a 100 percent chance you will lose. Oh, you might win at first. Everybody does. The smart ones quit while they are ahead and never gamble again. The rest of us, well . . . This is why they pay performers millions of dollars. It's not so much a paycheck, as it's a loan you pay back.

It was almost impossible for us to be at our best at two in the morning. The body does not like to get up that early to do anything, which is why SWAT teams all over America know that early in the morning is the safest time to deal with dangerous people because all you want to do is sleep. But we performed because we had to. Given a choice we would have passed. So the trick was to gamble a little just before showtime. We would get out of bed and hit the tables for about half an hour, and then we'd be jazzed up enough to do our show. The adrenaline rush did it for us. The trouble with that method was that after the show we'd be awake in Vegas and do what most people in Vegas do: gamble.

The Vegas gig kept us going financially as the touring wound down so we could shoot our first movie. Lou had made a deal with Paramount, where we would get around a million to do a Cheech and Chong movie. We hired Cheech's cousin Louie to help us write it and a guy named Floyd Mutrux to direct it. He also had a production office on Melrose Street where we would meet daily to write. Everything was good to go. The problem was that Cheech and I had never done a movie or worked with a movie director before.

The very first thing we learned is that we don't work well with other people. When we did the records we had to be alone so other people wouldn't throw their ideas into the mix. Our special brand of insanity was strictly between the two of us and could not be scripted, because so much of what we did was improvised. We would write down where we were going to do the bit, who would be in it, and what props we'd need. We wanted to take the same approach with our movie.

Floyd was a real movie director, and the director is god in the movie business. But this wasn't Floyd's movie, so as soon as we found out we couldn't work with him, the answer was clear: Lou would direct. After all, he produced our records and he understood our working style. So once that was settled we began work on *Cheech and Chong's Greatest Hits.*

I was charged with writing the scenes and sample dialogue. I would give the pages to Lou, who then had them typed and would distribute the script to all the department heads. We were rolling, as they say. Writing was comforting and I enjoyed the process, especially because I knew Cheech's character so well. Cheech and his cousin Louie had fun with my character; Louie designed the Stoner house down to the white wicker furniture.

Lou Adler had hired Robert Altman's crew, consisting of Lou Lombardo, editor and coproducer; Mike Moder, line producer; and Leon Ericksen, art director. We also worked with a couple of great casting directors, Fern Champion and Pam Basker. Preproduction went by pretty quickly, as Lou had a limited budget to work with so we had to start shooting right away. But before you shoot you have to have a cast, which is where Lou's Hollywood connection paid off. Robert Altman's people brought us Stacy Keach to play Sergeant Stadenko; Tom Skerritt to play the deranged Vietnam vet Strawberry; Strother Martin to play my dad Arnold Stoner; Edie Adams to play my mother, Mrs. Tempest Stoner; and Lupe Ontiveros to play Cheech's mother. We were surrounded by talented people who wanted to be in our movie. Jeff Goldblum came to the set just to meet us and see if there was a part we could use him in. And we used people Cheech and I had met over the years, such as June Fairchild, who played the Ajax lady who snorts Ajax cleaning powder thinking it was coke. I wanted to use Shelby as one of the girls who were hitchhiking who we pick up but she hadn't taken acting lessons yet so we settled on Zane Buzby and Wally Ann Wharton as the pill-popping, talkative, concert chicks. The parts of the gangsters were played by actors from Altman's stable: Val Avery and Ben Marino.

Once we had the cast we started shooting. The very first shot was me hitchhiking on PCH. Gathering for our first daily to watch everything shot on that day was a life-changing experience. Seeing yourself on the big screen is an ego boost. There you are: a movie star. I was enthralled with the image of me hitchhiking. It reminded me of a dark foreign movie, where you stay on the image for a long time, giving the audience time to study the character visually and get the backstory. Although the shot looked good to me, Adler and Lombardo were unhappy with the camera work and the guy who shot what I considered to be a great-looking piece of film was history, replaced by an older cameraman. Lou did not want a dark, brooding type of film. This was a comedy and it had to be bright.

So we forged ahead, this time shooting the scene where Cheech drives down PCH trying to pick up girls. The girls he was trying to pick up were unit manager Mike Moder's daughters. (Incidentally, Mike's son Danny is married to Julia Roberts.) Cheech's character, Pedro, was the classic lowrider guy from our live show. Chong was "everyman"; he was the rich, hippie kid from a wealthy family who rebelled against everything but lived at home so his family could support his rebel habits. It was the classic meeting of two cultures, where rich meets poor, Chicano meets hippie, yin meets yang, Cheech meets Chong.

The dialogue was improvised but we had been testing it for years in our live show. So it was rehearsed improvisation with a good deal of pot added to the mix to keep everything funny. Cheech and I shared a trailer so we could work on the movie during lunch breaks and setup breaks. I never stopped writing the entire movie because we were writing it as we went along. Each scene had our undivided attention and it showed on-screen.

There was one scene where Cheech wakes up and pees into the clothes hamper that was added at the last minute. I had not written it into the script, so the crew was in the midst of tearing down the set when we realized we had not shot the hamper scene. We had everyone redo the set, rolled camera, and got it on one take. Thank Jesus, because that is one of the most memorable scenes in the movie. The scene where Cheech is awoken by the kids watching cartoons and eating their Cheerios was a reenactment of Robbi and Rae Dawn when they were seven and nine and woke up Cheech, who was crashing on the sofa. We used our real experiences in the movie, which in a way, made it a sort of precursor to reality shows in America, with pot as the object of our affections.

The cast and crew (but mainly the crew) were having a ball shooting our movie because of the freedom associated with it. We breezed through the shooting schedule, because whenever we ran into something that didn't work we scrapped it and moved on to gags that *did* work. I wrote a touching scene in which Cheech and the Stoner have a conversation in Cheech's home at night while everyone else is sound asleep. It never made the cut because it stopped the movie's momentum. Another scene that hit the cutting-room floor was an exchange between my character's father (Strother Martin) and me at the prison. I wanted to do an homage to *Rebel Without a Cause*, the classic James Dean movie, but it slowed the pace, too.

Many of the movie bits were also written by Adler and Lombardo, such as the bird that is blown up at Strawberry's house, the dead dog at the border crossing, the nuns who are searched by Stadenko, and much of Stadenko's clowning around and farce acting. I wanted his scenes to be more realistic, but that would have made the movie too artsy and we were going for a more commercial feel in order to make more money. As we neared the ending of the movie I felt pretty good about the end result. I was a little miffed at being left out of Stadenko's scene at the motel, in which he gives his men a pep talk about the big drug shipment coming in from Mexico. I had been on the set during the rest of the film (except for the car chase scenes), and I was practically codirecting the movie along with Cheech and Lou. But the motel room was small, someone had to go, and it turned out to be me.

I couldn't help but notice, however, that the closer we came to finishing the movie, the less involved I became. Lou seemed to have gotten his legs as a director during filming and had taken over. Cheech felt the change as well. Cheech told me that Lou suggested he be more "Cheech." Although it was a simple suggestion it wasn't the direction Cheech was looking for. But, hey, Lou had never directed a movie before. In fact, his abilities were in the music recording business, where he excelled. The

music for the song that Cheech sang at the battle of the punk
bands, "Earache My Eye," was written by guitarist Gaye Delorme. He came up with the now famous riff and the first line,
"Mama talking to me."

The song was made special by Lou Adler, who turned all our
music recordings into a who's who of the music industry, and
"Earache My Eye" was no different. Gaye Delorme was flown in
from Vancouver to play guitar on the track, with Airto Moreira,
the famous percussionist from Brazil, on the drums. Airto was
brought to America to play with the great Miles Davis and was
considered one of the top drummers on the scene. He became
very close with Cheech and me and would visit with his wife
Flora Purim, the jazz vocalist, and their little girl during the
seventies. We recorded the music at A&M Studios on La Brea
and Sunset and mixed it in our little mix-down room, where we
created some mixing magic by inserting the guitar solo in the
middle and taking part of Gaye's solo and making it an introduction to the song. The lyrics really spoke volumes to the bud-
ding punk-rock scene that was just beginning in Los Angeles.
Having comedians like Cheech and Chong as the spokespeople
for that generation was way too cool for everyone. We were
cool because unlike other comics we never made fun of the
culture from a stand-up's perspective. We were the characters
who everyone could look down on; therefore, we were the culture. The material has withstood the test of time: *Up in Smoke*
is still popular after thirty years as is "Earache My Eye," the tune
to which everyone in America knows the first three bars of the
riff (da da da, da da da dun dun dun).

But the truth is *Up in Smoke* almost did not get released.
Paramount saw a rough cut and hated it to the point that they
gave it back to Lou and told him he would have to put up his
own money from now on. They were not giving him another

dime. The scene at the Roxy was supposed to be the end. We have the battle of the bands and the van made of pot burns up. The smoke from the van gets everyone in Los Angeles high, including airline pilots who are in the process of landing planes. The smoke filters into everyone's home and the effects are hilarious—and expensive. Too expensive, which is why Lou Lombardo and Lou Adler come up with their own ending.

The ending they surprised me with was in effect a "this was all a dream" ending. Remember when we were in the lowrider, the love machine, and it's filled with smoke from us puffing on the joint? Well, they cut back to that scene and when the smoke clears you see Sergeant Stadenko dressed in a blue cop uniform peeking in the back window. This is supposed to tell the audience that we imagined everything that happened from the time the cop stopped us until the battle of the bands. It sucked. When I saw the new ending, I was surprised all right. I was surprised I kept my mouth shut and didn't stand up and yell, "What the fuck did you do to our movie?"

When the suits from Paramount filed past us after the screening, it felt like we were at a funeral. We were in some ways. Our movie and our movie career was in the casket being lowered into the ground. I have always hated "it was all a dream" bullshit endings because they imply that the fantasy we took you on was not real. The joints we smoked were not marijuana joints but joints made of tobacco from India that have no nicotine in them because Cheech and I don't smoke cigarettes. It's like telling the audience, "Thanks for your money, but fuck you." It was such an insult. We had a postmortem at the Top of the Roxs to discuss our next step.

"Well, what did you think of the ending?" Lou Adler asked me in a low voice. Lou Lombardo was standing close so he could hear my reaction.

"It doesn't work," I replied. I wanted to say how I really felt but I was still in shock. "We need to shoot another ending," I added. I felt my power return to me with that statement. I knew we needed another ending and I was the only one who could write it. I would describe what I envisioned to Cheech, who would then add his twists to the dialogue and we would be good to go.

Lou Adler started to tell me that Paramount would not give us the money, but Lou Lombardo cut him off and asked, "How do you see the movie ending, Tommy?"

"Well, I know its not all a dream. I know that for sure. Let Cheech and I talk about it and we will come up with an ending."

Lou Adler was not happy with my suggestion, but Lou Lombardo knew I was right—we needed another ending.

Cheech and I talked the next day and we came up with a simple solution. Continue the dream sequence. Don't end it until the dream has a happy ending. You need an uplifting ending for a comedy. That goes back to the first Westerns, where the hero finally gets the girl and the horse nudges the cowboy into her arms for the last kiss hidden by his huge cowboy hat. You want the audience walking out of the theater with a smile on their faces. This is the art of popular filmmaking.

Lou Adler and I became estranged after that screening because I wouldn't tell him what the ending was going to be. I told him that I had to direct it myself. The Immigration scene in which the place where we are rehearsing is raided by Immigration officials, or "La Migra," was one of the themes in our records. Cheech's Chicano lowrider character was acceptable to the Latino community because it rang true. *Up in Smoke* also rang true and that is why it went on to become the biggest grossing movie of the year it was released. And it was because we fought so hard to protect its authenticity that Lou Adler and I split. Lou wanted to make *Cheech and Chong's Greatest Hits*, but instead we made *Up in Smoke*.

We changed the name of the movie because when Lou didn't need me on the set or in the editing room, I had picked up my guitar and written the tune "Up in Smoke" and sang it for Cheech and Lou Adler. Cheech immediately jumped up and said, "That's the title of the movie!" Then he wrote a Spanish version of the song and Lou recorded it with a full orchestra and background singers.

Writing and singing the song on my own was a departure from our usual routine; Cheech and I would always write everything together and then show Lou. But I wrote the song alone to define myself as a writer. I came to realize I was not getting the respect I deserved as a screenwriter. I also realized that no one was going to jump up and say, "Oh, look, Tommy is writing the script, let's give him money and credit." Hollywood is brutal when it comes to giving credit where credit is due. I once heard that a record executive received an award for a re-release of a collection of an old jazz guitarist's tunes. He thanked the people for the award and mentioned his "hard work" but never once mentioned the man whose work he was exploiting. The executive acted as if he had written and recorded the tunes. Unbelievable.

We shot the new ending with me directing. The editors put the movie together and released it in the fall of 1978. It was a smash hit. *Up in Smoke* became the most successful movie of 1978 and Lou Adler is down on the credits as the director. So Lou did something right. Movie theaters all over the world wanted prints. Drive-in theaters played the movie for more than a year straight. It played in Paris at a theater for ten years straight. But as I said, the film's success also brought conflict between Lou Adler and me.

Cheech and I had to take off the couple of months it took to shoot the movie, and our income had fallen dangerously low. We had to hit the concert trail and promote the movie at the same time. The press junket for *Up in Smoke* was a nightmare; we had to travel from city to city, answering questions from many journalists about this hit movie we wrote, codirected, and starred in. And we were getting short-changed money-wise. It was a strange position to be in. Usually when we went on the road, we came home with a nice paycheck. This time Cheech and I were promoting, at our expense, a product that everyone else was making money off of. It did not make sense so I started to talk shit about the entire process. I was angry and hurt at the lousy deal we were getting. I was also suffering from the inflated ego that comes with making and being responsible for a successful movie. I was the only one who said we needed a new ending. No one else stood up and said the "it's all a dream" scenario was a shit ending. Cheech agreed with me but he never said anything until I said it. Lou Adler sure didn't say anything because I think he sincerely liked the ending that he and Lou Lombardo came up with. No, I was the guy who felt cheated and betrayed, so I spoke out and told anyone who would listen. Unfortunately, the who was my audience and soon reports of my unhappiness filtered back to Lou.

We were doing the Aladdin gig in Vegas when I received a call from Lou. He had read what I was saying, and he wasn't happy. So I told him how I felt. I wanted a better deal for Cheech and myself. He asked me what type of deal would make me happy and I said, "Let's split the movie three ways." I had no way of knowing he had already made a deal with Paramount stipulating that if he put up his money to finish the movie, he would own the rights. There was no way he was going to change that deal.

The truth is I wasn't concerned with the deal when we were creating the movie, because I trusted Lou to take care of us as he did with our record deal. We never negotiated record deals because he owned the record company. He put up all the money for the production of the albums. We worked for him and he always made sure we got the best of everything. I felt, however, that the movie business leveled the playing field. He was new to the business. We were new to the business. We were the stars. We deserved to be treated like stars. But he would not budge. He said we could go thirds on the next movie, but this one was going to stay the way it was. So I told him, "I guess that means Cheech and I are moving on." And he said, "I guess that's what it means." And that was the end of our relationship with Lou Adler.

CHAPTER FOURTEEN

EXIT LOU,
ENTER HOWARD

Los Angeles, California, 1979

When I told Cheech what had happened with Lou, he was quiet. He was as broke as I was, since we had stopped touring to make the movie; he just looked concerned. He never blamed me for not consulting with him before leaving Lou, but he was pissed off because we were doing the press junket on our dollar.

Things didn't look very good for us. But we did have a hit movie, and the publicity from the movie packed every venue we played from then on. The problem was we had tasted the movie life and we liked the taste. The concert life was coming to a fast close, because fans of the movie did not want to buy into our live act anymore. They sat there waiting for us to shut up so they could yell *Up in Smoke* references.

I asked Cheech to talk to his friend Geraldo Rivera to see if he knew of a lawyer who could get us out of the contract with Lou so we could do another movie. Rivera suggested we meet with a securities lawyer named Leo Kizer. We met with Leo in New York at the Yale Club, where he was a member, and told him our story. Leo told us that he would attack Lou from a securities angle because that was his specialty. He also asked for a ten-thousand-dollar deposit. It wasn't an unusual request, but it didn't seem worth it to me. How could he get us free on a security issue? Weird.

In the meantime, Lou's cousin Marshall Blonstein was all torn up about our break with Lou. Marshall was our biggest fan. And he got us the airplay for our records and was as much a part of our success as anyone. He loved Cheech and Chong and he wanted to help in any way he could. So he found a businessman from New York who had written a book about how to be successful in Hollywood. The guy was a neighbor of his and he wanted us to meet him. We had secured a gig at the Comedy Store for a week straight. Mitzi, the owner and founder of the Store, had talked to our booking agent, and we made a deal where we got the door and she took the bar for two shows a night for a week. It was a gig to remember. The place was sold out almost immediately because of the movie and because Cheech and I rarely performed in Los Angeles, so the people were ready for a Cheech and Chong fix. Pauly Shore told me recently that he sat in the light booth and watched us perform. The audience was the elite of Hollywood entertainers. Richard Pryor came and met us as we left the stage. It was the ultimate sign of respect from one of the greatest standup comics who ever lived. Seeing Richard that night validated our career. It was as if the Pope came and blessed us as we left the stage. Marshall's neighbor and friend was also there with his wife. And after saying our thank-yous to the many celebrities, we were introduced to Howard Brown and his lovely wife, Eva. The Browns stood out even in that crowd. Howard was about 5'6", balding, and very New York Jewish gangster–looking, while Eva was at least 6', blonde, Swedish beauty queen–like, and had been Miss Sweden at one time. She was wearing a form-fitting dress that clung to every delicious curve of her body. Her face was to die for, as they say in New York.

For some reason Cheech took an immediate dislike to Howard. Why? I will never know. I asked myself that question for years and I actually asked Cheech but he never gave me a reason. He just never liked or trusted Howard. On the other hand, I loved the guy. I could relate to his wannabe-gangster ways because I grew up with the same people in Vancouver and Calgary. All the hip, rich guys in Calgary and Vancouver were Jewish. And I respected them because they were always there when I needed them. These were the guys who helped us get the Shanghai Junk, where Cheech and I created our act. A guy named Georgie Bier handed me a handful of cash for the down payment on the club. No one else would do that. Not the banks, that's for sure. And when Cheech and I decided to head south and become stars, we went to another Jewish guy named Lionel Shapiro, who handed us enough for the plane fare: no paper, nothing but a promise to pay it back when we made it big. Cheech and Chong would not have existed had it not been for my Jewish friends. So when Cheech decided he did not want anything to do with Howard, I tried my best to convince him. But he told me that if I was going to go with Howard, he was going to take his money and go with someone he trusted. And that is exactly what he did. We split what we had and created our separate accounting systems with separate accountants.

Howard was gracious and understanding when I told him how Cheech felt. What Cheech didn't know was that the gangster look was just a front. Howard was an intellectual nerd in real life, who had degrees in business and accounting. He had also been one of the youngest board members of the New York Stock Exchange. He had balls and he had accounting chops that to this day I still use. He took a look at Shelby and my money situation and immediately showed us how to arrange our finances, how to pay our taxes, and how to budget our daily expenses. Shelby loved Howard because he encouraged her to take over paying bills and handling our money. Up until then we had accountants who were connected with Lou handling our bills. This was a mistake that we rectified immediately.

On the movie front, we found out that Lou had options on our next movie and we also learned that even though Paramount had a huge hit with *Up in Smoke*, they did not want to do our next movie. In fact, when the movie was number one across the nation, they offered us half a million for the next one. That was the same amount we got for *Up in Smoke*. Thankfully, Howard knew the movie business. He had worked with Howard Koch, a respected movie producer whose credits included *The Manchurian Candidate* and *The Odd Couple*, and he also had a commercial production company for a while. But Howard's biggest asset was he was connected. Hollywood is a funny town; it is really all about who you know. The Larry David show *Curb Your Enthusiasm* is a great example of how Hollywood works. The Jewish community is very tribal inasmuch as they socialize and do business at the same time. And Howard was a made man in the Jewish community in Hollywood.

So over Cheech's objections, Howard went to work and freed us from Lou Adler and got us the second movie deal. That was his goal. Howard taught me to set goals, to know where I was going and know what I wanted. We talked about what we wanted to accomplish, and I told him I wanted to do another Cheech and Chong movie and that I wanted to direct it. That's all. Another movie.

Howard asked if it would be possible for me to do the next movie with Lou, and when I said no, he told me the first thing I needed was an entertainment lawyer. I told him about Leo Kizer and he asked, "Is he an entertainment lawyer?"

"No, he is a securities lawyer," I replied.

"Well, when you get into trouble with securities, then we call Leo. However, because you want to do another movie and you need to be cut loose from Lou, we need a good entertainment lawyer. I will get you a list of all the entertainment lawyers in town and you choose one."

The next day Howard called and told me to come to his office in Century City for a meeting. He had a list of lawyers.

"Who do you like?" I asked, looking over the names.

"I like them all," he replied. "But it has to be your choice."

"Why can't you choose for me?" I countered.

"Because I am not you," he replied.

"Then what would you do?" I asked.

"If I were in your shoes? I would do it myself. Personally, I never pay lawyers. I call them up and ask them, off the record, what they would do regarding whatever problem I have. They tell me honestly and I thank them for their advice. Then I hire a young up-and-coming lawyer and tell him what to do. That's what I would do. But I am not you. You are a star and you need proper representation. You need an entertainment lawyer, so pick one."

I looked at the list and the name Eric Wiessman and Associates caught my eye. The next day Cheech and I were sitting in Eric's office discussing our case. Cheech was in a good mood because he could relate to Eric and Stan Coleman, Eric's junior attorney, who looked like one of his old frat brothers. I sat there listening and felt really good about getting our own legal representation.

The first thing Eric did was to contact Lou's attorney, and the two lawyers began talking about how to move forward. In the meantime, Howard was busy networking. Howard played basketball and, like us, was addicted to it. He played every Saturday morning in an outdoor high school court in Beverly Hills, where the players had to climb a fence to get to the court because the gates to the playground were locked on the weekends. So every Saturday morning power men in the entertainment business would climb a chain-link fence and play three-on-three basketball for a few hours. This is where Howard would talk business in between games with the executives. Nothing specific, just business gossip: who is doing what, who is looking for product, who could greenlight a movie and who couldn't, what guy is on his way out and who is going to replace him. It was good to know this information because it helped Howard plan a strategy to help him sell the next Cheech and Chong movie.

I was getting an education in the art of the movie deal. *Up in Smoke* was still kicking ass in theaters so things were good and getting better. Then the day came when we settled with Lou. He retained rights to the characters Pedro and Man, but we owned Cheech and Chong outright. We were free to deal with anyone for the next movie.

Howard immediately set up a meeting with Ned Tanin, the president of Universal. Ned was a friend of Howard's and a fan of Cheech and Chong going back to when he was the head of a powerful agency that handled all the big stars in the business. Howard called me before the meeting and asked what Cheech and I would be satisfied with. Paramount had offered us half a million between the two of us, so I told Howard if we got a million I'd be happy. Half a million each was a lot of money. Howard said he would try and went off to meet with Ned on the Universal lot.

We planned to meet afterward at the Hamburger Hamlet on Sunset near Doheny at one PM. I arrived at 12:30 and was waiting in a booth when a waiter came up and asked me if I was

Tommy Chong. I said I was and he told me that I had a telephone call. So I followed the waiter to the telephone and knowing it was Howard, I asked, "How did we do?"

It took a second for Howard to answer and at first my heart sank when he said, "I couldn't get the million." I waited for the next blow, but instead Howard's voice rose a little and said, "I got you two. Plus eight million for the budget."

I thought, *That's right, the budget! We never discussed the budget.* "OK, I am going to call Cheech." I was about to hang up the phone, when Howard yelled, "Wait, wait . . . there's more."

I was stunned. Howard paused, waiting for me to regroup before continuing: "The meeting with Ned was only like a half hour, so I had the secretary at Ned's call Frank Price at Columbia. Frank wants the next two pictures after Universal."

I was stunned. This was way too much for me to handle. I sat down because my knees were weak from excitement. Howard went on to explain that the two movies after Universal would be for three million and four in fees, plus the eight-million-dollar budget.

"They are going to pay you and Cheech fifty thousand dollars each to show up at a meeting and tell them three stories. They will pick two, and those two stories will become the two movies after Universal."

I called Cheech and relayed the good news to him. He, of course, could not believe what I was telling him and kept saying, "He got us two million with Universal? I thought he was going to talk to Paramount. Wow, that's great! So what does Howard get out of this deal?"

I thought, *Man, you still don't trust this guy, do you?*

"He gets 10 percent."

Cheech thought for a moment. "Ten percent?"

Then I added, "That's 10 percent from each of us making Howard's take 20 percent." Howard had only asked for 10 percent total because that was the usual amount that an agent or a manager would be entitled to; however, because he had far exceeded what we had expected to get I felt he honestly deserved 20 percent. Cheech agreed and I had the privilege of going back and telling Howard, "Listen man, I couldn't get you 10 percent . . . I got you 20 percent!" And, of course, Howard was very pleased we were so generous.

It was interesting to see what each of us did with our newfound wealth. Howard immediately spent his 20 percent on a ranch-style house in Encino in the Valley and he paid cash. He was through paying rent and wanted financial freedom from the monthly nut that he paid and got nothing in return by way of investment.

Howard encouraged Cheech and me to buy an office building across from the Warner Bros lot but Cheech did not want anything to do with Howard, so we missed a huge opportunity. I should have bought it myself, but I never had the vision that Howard had so I also missed out.

I hired an attorney by the name of Joe Mannis to act as my manager. Joe also turned us on to an accountant named Bob Mitchell and together they invested our new wealth, putting most of it into a retirement fund. Cheech hired Stan Coleman, the lawyer who Howard had obtained for us to split with Lou, and an accountant named Betty Bell. So now we were represented to the hilt and we proceeded to make the projects that Howard had secured for us.

The Universal picture was the first order of business, so Howard obtained a suite of offices and we went to work writing the movie. Everyone in the office and at Universal kept referring to it as *Cheech and Chong's Next Movie.* The title stuck and we eventually released it under that name. The major change this time around was that I would be the sole director. This was due to Howard's persistence with the studios and with me. I wanted the job. I did not want to go through the pain of watching someone else screw up my vision. I knew what Cheech and Chong were capable of and I was determined to get it all on-screen. I did call Terry Malick, the director of *Badlands* and, in my humble opinion, the greatest American film director of all time. He answered the phone and when I asked if he would be interested in directing our next movie he asked who had written it. When I said I did, he told me I should direct it myself. He went on to tell me what I had already known: "No one can read your mind—if it's your vision, then you have to see it through yourself." I thanked him for his time and decided direct it my-self after all.

Even though I had never directed a motion picture, I had written and directed Cheech and Chong for more than ten years now and that was more experience than many first-time direc-tors had. And besides, I knew from *Up in Smoke* that the key to a successful movie lies with the crew, the editors, and most im-portant, the director of photography. Universal provided the other missing link, the unit manager.

Enter Peter Macgregor-Scott. Peter was a veteran of the film business, having done at least fifty films before he met me. The unit manager handles the nuts and bolts of the movie, from determining locations (with the director) to deciding how many dressing room trucks are needed on a given day. He also helps with the shooting schedule, juggling shoots to fit actors, weather, availability of sets, and so on. He doles out huge sums of cash daily and has to keep track of every penny while scouting locations, arranging transportation for cast and crew, and feeding everyone three meals a day. Peter's first job was to get me into the Director's Guild. He tried to get Alfred Hitchcock to sign my recommendation card, but old Hitch was . . . too old. He found someone who was a fan and I was good to go.

Cheech and I met every day during the preproduction, working on the script and having lunch in the Universal dining room, where we would see the various actors and the boss himself having lunch. Lew Wasserman was the big honcho at the time and he would preside over lunch like a headmaster at a boarding school.

John Belushi and Dan Aykroyd were on the lot shooting *The Blues Brothers* with John Landis directing, so we saw Belushi quite a bit. He would get stoned and roam the Universal lot, terrorizing unsuspecting people by showing up unannounced and insisting they listen to his favorite punk band. John was a big guy and when he wanted you to listen to his tape there was no escaping him. John would burst into offices past startled secretaries with his tape blaring as he enthusiastically danced and played air guitar.

We did preproduction on the script until we were ready to shoot. The problem was we needed the go-ahead from Ned. We had been paid, the script was ready, we had the cast and crew lined up, but we needed Ned to officially say that the movie was a go. Howard Brown, Cheech, and I descended on Ned's office, but he refused to say yes. It was weird. Hollywood movie executives have an aversion to saying yes. It's not a part of their vocabulary. They can say no all day—and they do—but try getting a simple yes out of them and it's a nightmare. Ned walked around his office like a caged animal looking for an escape route.

"Ned, are we good to go?" Howard was stalking him, while Cheech and I tried to cut off his escape route. "Come on, Ned, say the word."

"OK . . ." And with that Ned stormed out of his office, leaving us there looking at one another.

"Was that 'OK, it's a go'?" Howard asked. "I would say it wasn't a no, so it's a go, guys!"

The first day of shooting was a historical moment for all of us, including the director of photography, King Baggot. When Peter came to me with a list of DPs, I asked him who he would choose.

"Well, mate, they can all do the job," he said in his English accent. "It really comes down to who you are comfortable with."

I thought for a moment. Then I got an idea: *Get a new guy. Someone who will be so happy to get the job that he will kill for you.* It made sense. You don't want an old pro who has seen everything and will be bored watching you learn your job. I decided to find a cameraman who wanted to become a DP. That's the kind of guy I wanted.

King Baggot was a cameraman whose specialty was the steady cam. A steady cam operator has a camera strapped to his body, allowing him to follow actors upstairs and around corners, eliminating time-consuming setups with dolly tracks and lights. It took a strong man who was in good shape to lug around the camera and keep it trained on the actors without falling or banging into the set. The steady cam operator's assistant guides him and protects him from danger. King was studying to be a DP and so when Peter approached him with our job offer he jumped all over it. King was also able to direct the action, so Cheech and I could concentrate on acting in front of the camera.

We started early on the first day. I met the crew and we went to work, moving from one setup to another until, at the end of the day, we had shot forty-two setups. It was an unheard of number for a first day. Usually you are lucky if you get five set-ups because everyone is usually meeting for the first time and the nature of the business dictates you take your time so the overtime and money flows in. Millions of dollars are available and if you finish too fast you don't get to use all the money. No one gets a pat on the back for finishing early and under budget. No one.

The movie was coming along. We spent quite a few days on the back lot of a movie set equipped with lower-middle class homes. Cheech and I lived in one raggedy house with broken plumbing next to a single, very angry, gay man who resented that people like Cheech and Chong actually existed. The neighbor was a former child star who had been reduced to doing bit roles wherever and whenever he could. He carried a little dog wherever he went and was so mean I thought he was perfect for the role of the neighbor. Doing scenes with him was a different matter.

Neatnik (the neighbor) and Cheech were in a scene in which Cheech ignores Neatnik and instead looks at some treasure he stole from the movie studio where he works. It was getting close to lunch and everyone wanted to finish the scene so they could break for lunch, but Neatnik wanted to go over the scene with me. He really wanted attention because he was a star once and he was used to getting all the attention, especially from the director. Neatnik was in the middle of some minor question when King started giving instructions and moving people around to get a better angle on the shot. Neatnik started to go ballistic and King, unaware of the problem, ignored Neatnik completely and continued to move people around. Cheech was also hungry and tired of doing the scene, so he muttered something to Neatnik under his breath but Neatnik heard him. His face and bald head got red and he stormed off in a huff. "I'll be in my trailer!" he shouted as he left.

Peter immediately sensed danger and asked, "What got his tail in a knot?"

"I told him to fuck off," Cheech answered in his nonchalant manner, as if saying that to someone like Neatnik was a good way to shoot a movie, especially knowing we could not replace Neatnik without having to reshoot everything we had done during the last few days. The cast and crew broke for lunch, while Peter and I tried to talk the guy down.

"He wants an apology and his dressing room filled with champagne and flowers," Peter said. "What should we do?"

I thought for a second and then told Peter, "Do what he says."

Peter looked at me with a glint in his eye. I had made the right decision. It was the only decision. We were spending about a hundred thousand a day shooting the film and if it took a few bottles of booze and some flowers to keep the train rolling, so be it. Cheech also apologized and, in the end, Neatnik became a great guy to work with and did the rest of the shoot without a peep.

Cheech played two roles in *Next Movie:* his main character and his cousin Red, a character from our live act who did outrageous bits. I never got tired of watching that character. Cheech would transform himself into this bumbling, good-natured, good old boy who made you forget he was actually a Mexican playing the role of a redneck. When I see the Blue Collar Comics onstage making millions of dollars, I flash back to the time when Cheech played a redneck.

The scene I am the most proud of is the scene in the unemployment office in which Cheech makes out with Donna while I watch Michael Winslow make crazy faces and sounds. An old geezer, played by Malcolm Drummond, and a junkie, played by Tony Vascaria (the heroin addict who was once married to Lenny Bruce's mother) were also in the scene. The junkie nods off while the old geezer focuses on his cigarette ash, which gets longer and longer. I was told that some film schools show that scene as an example of how much can go on in one scene. It took one take.

Being a director required from me many responsibilities, but it provided me with many perks, one being that I could cast whomever I chose. I wanted to cast Shelby in *Up in Smoke*, but Lou was the director and I didn't have the authority to do so. *Next Movie* was different. I was about to cast Shelby when I realized how that would look, especially to Cheech, who supported my decision to be the director but did not want Shelby in our movie. Instead I cast Rikki, Cheech's wife, in a major role. Rikki was beautiful, had a model-thin body, and had been taking acting lessons—so in she went.

Next I made a few trips down to the Groundlings Theatre on Melrose and used talent from there to cast the remaining roles. The Groundlings Theatre was and still is one of the best places to find new talent, as it is home to some of the best actors in Los Angeles. Seeing as Cheech and I acquired our comedy skills secondhand from improvisation theaters, it was only natural that we cast the movie there.

Paul Reubens was our first choice because he was the funniest original talent I had ever seen. His character Pee-wee Herman came to life as a separate entity and went on to become an icon in the entertainment business. His television show, *Pee-wee's Playhouse,* ruled the airwaves until Paul was busted for lewd conduct by an undercover policeman in a porno theater.

Apparently, Paul was caught masturbating in the theater. Duh! It's a porno theater! That's what they are there for! But the bust stopped the Pee-wee Herman express train to fame in its tracks. And Paul's career was damaged to the point that Pee-wee, our beloved Pee-wee, stopped performing. It was a Hollywood scandal that evoked memories of the Hollywood of the twenties when stars like Fatty Arbuckle were treated in a similar fashion. It was a classic case of building them up just to tear them down.

But the Pee-wee we discovered was young and pure and full of talent. It was as if Paul and Pee-wee were totally different people, and Paul was there representing Pee-wee as his agent. Once we cast Paul, we tapped Edie McClurg to play the part of Rikki's mom. Edie had been in other movies, most notably as the bad girl opposite Sissy Spacek in *Carrie*. Edie was perfect for the role of the wealthy mom from a fancy home who goes on an adventure with Red, Chong, and Rikki after getting stoned in a car while on their way to a comedy club. Looking back on it now, this scene was genius because it became a comedy within the comedy. They were stoned and on their way to a comedy club, telling stupid jokes that everyone in the audience, who would probably also be stoned, can laugh at a joke within a joke. *Up in Smoke* was the story of two guys who meet and go on a quest for dope, while riding around in a van made of dope. *Next Movie* was the story of three guys (with Cheech playing two characters) on a quest for laughs because they have all the dope they need.

Cheech's main character in *Next Movie* worked at a movie studio, which enabled us to show spoofs of popular television shows at the time, such as *The Incredible Hulk*. Lou Ferrigno played the Hulk on TV, but we used the Universal Studios amusement park Hulk, played by Jake from Body by Jake, who happened to be a friend of mine from the gym. I used quite a few of my friends from the gym in all the movies; in fact, I have met more actors in gyms than I have at movie screenings. I knew Jake before I got into directing and we always talked, so when he landed a job as the Incredible Hulk for the Universal Studios amusement park, I wrote a bit in which Jake is lost, looking for the phony brick wall to burst through when he runs into Cheech, who directs him to the wrong wall. Meanwhile, Charlie's Angels are yelling, "Help me, Wamba," creating another spoof within a spoof. (One of the "Help me, Wamba" girls was Rita Wilson, Tom Hanks's wife and a fine talented actress in her own right. I saw Rita recently and she reminded me that she was one of the girls in that scene.)

There were many memorable moments in that movie, but the one moment I will always remember is when the Blues Brothers show up on our set. John Landis drove them over to see us one afternoon while we were taking a break from filming. We had just wrapped up a scene in which I go to use the toilet only to find it broken and piled high with shit. I proceed to pee off our porch and onto the neighbor's garden. The joke lies in the contrast between our raggedy junky house and the neighbor's totally neat and prissy house, and the fact that I pee on his property shows the disrespect we have for order. To film the pee scene, we had a grip hold a water hose off camera. Dan Aykroyd and John Belushi gathered around the monitor as we watched the shot we'd just filmed. The grip who was holding the hose was upset because you could see the hose for a split second. I couldn't see the gaff at first, but the video operator slowed it down so I could see the hose and the guy's hand. I was about to redo the shot when Dan Aykroyd said, "That shot works because it looks like you're holding your dick." After watching the shot in real time I realized Dan was right. The gaff flashed onscreen so briefly that only the seasoned eye of a camera operator would be able to tell it was a mistake—a stoned audience would certainly not. So it stayed in the picture, and we moved on. As brief as it was, it was a thrill being directed by Dan, whom I consider a comic genius and music legend.

We moved off the lot and into Hollywood to shoot the scene where Red inadvertently clears the titty bar when he uses his ghetto blaster to simulate police sirens. Red's character was based on a real guy from the bush who I'd met in Vancouver. He was a uranium prospector and lived alone in the mountains for eleven months of the year. When he would come to town he would bring his loner mindset with him. He was a wild man in a civilized setting. He had thousands of dollars in cash that he had to spend before going back the bush, so the first thing he bought was a '38 Chevy four-door sedan that he paid way too much for. He then purchased three boxes of oranges that he stuffed in the back of his car. He craved oranges while he was in the bush so he would buy as many as he could. He drove around eating oranges until he needed gas. At the gas station, he decided he needed to wash his car, so he took the hose used for filling radiators, took off his shoes, rolled up his pants, and began to do it himself. The service station owner saw what he was doing and told him to get out. The bushman totally ignored him and continued washing his car. The station owner had his staff try to force him to leave, but when they opened the back door to move the car themselves, oranges spilled out onto the station area and street. The staff was falling all over themselves while the bushman continued to wash his car. This very same bushman came to the club where we were performing and threw a handful of quarters at us as we did the show. We were playing music and picking up money at the same time.

One of the things Red collected was sounds. The bush has only wild sounds: birds, rain, and other such sounds of nature. Red missed the city sounds: sounds of people living and moving about, sounds of traffic, police sirens, bullhorns, and gunfire. So he recorded and collected sounds with his ghetto blaster—just like the character does in the titty bar scene in *Next Movie*.

Cheech and I had some good laughs making this movie. Cheech wrote a biker guitar solo and designed a great set for it. This is the scene where I am playing a guitar so loudly that it disturbs the entire neighborhood. Dogs cover their ears with their paws. People stop in their tracks and react to the noise. Cheech comes home and tries to open the door, but the music is so loud that he has to fight the sound waves as he is flattened by the volume. He finally opens the door and tries to turn off the amplifiers, but the sound blast pushes him backward. I am totally oblivious to the havoc I am causing. My eyes are closed and I am grooving to my music, as I wail away on a guitar that has a motorcycle kickstand as a tremo bar. Cheech finally pulls the plug and remarks, "I hope I can still have kids."

This scene was only one of the many crazy scenes that made *Next Movie* such a force in the film world. I originally planned to use more animation in the movie but I soon learned it was best to not mix the genres. We found our animator in Vince's Gym on Ventura Boulevard, near Lankershim. Vince's Gym was home to a few Hollywood actors, like Robert Blake and Erik Estrada. I discovered Vince through his writing in muscle magazines. Vince was one of the most knowledgeable men in the fitness industry. He hated steroids and would not allow anyone who took them to work out at his gym. He was totally Mr. Natural and I credit Vince with helping me craft and shape my body. He got me in great shape for the movies and gave hope to the many pot smokers who saw that a pothead could have a nice body, too.

We were working out at Vince's when a stocky little guy came over and introduced himself to Cheech. "I'm Paul Power and I did a comic strip of you guys when you were in Australia."

Cheech looked at Paul for a moment and said, "Man, we have been looking for you. Yeah, ever since we saw your comic strip we have been wanting to talk to you."

I was busy doing triceps exercises when Cheech walked over with Paul and said, "Look who I found." Cheech told me who he was and I immediately hired Paul to do the animation work on *Next Movie*. Although Paul is 5'3" in heels, he is also a martial arts expert in judo and has been in some major fights in his career—mostly back-alley fights. He is a tough little fucker and a fantastic animator and artist. I still work with Paul today. And Cheech collaborated with Paul some years ago in *Cheech the Bus Driver,* Cheech's children's book.

While *Next Movie* was being edited, Cheech and I met with the heads of Columbia Pictures to pitch our next two films. This was the meeting that Howard had written into the contract— Cheech and I got a hundred grand just to show up and give them three stories from which they would pick two. I had totally forgotten about the meeting until Howard reminded me that it was to take place immediately. I had not even told Cheech until the day of the meeting. When we met outside the Columbia offices, Cheech asked me what stories we were going to tell them. I told Cheech that I had a few plot lines I was working on we'd have to just improvise.

When we entered the office we were met by Sherry Lansing, a stunningly beautiful ex-model who eventually became president of Paramount; Marvin Antonouski; and Frank Price, the president of Columbia. Howard made the introductions and as we shook hands and said hello, we were each handed a check for fifty thousand dollars, as per the agreement. I did not understand the concept of the bonus until years later and countless attempts to get a project greenlit. Only then did I see the genius behind the money. The bonus meant that the studio was serious and was actually going to make the movies. Most movie deals fall through the cracks because the powers that be say no.

Hollywood is a "no" town. People in the business listen and say no or "let me run this by somebody else." The reason for the automatic no is to see how much the producer is behind his or her own project. The studio executive's job is to poke holes in the project, find the weaknesses. *Star Wars* and *E.T.* were both turned down by studios. Everyone gets turned down. This is why getting the bonus for a meeting showed Howard's sheer genius. And this, folks, was after we were in effect turned down by the studio that was enjoying the benefits of a number one box office smash that we wrote, codirected, and starred in.

I told three stories in the Columbia offices that day, and my most attentive audience member was Cheech, who was hearing them for the first time. I was basically making them up as I went along. My improvisational skills certainly came in handy at that moment. I only recall one of the three stories I told.

The first story was based on the Peter Principle, which is failing upward. The Peter Principle dictates that incompetence should be rewarded. The story had Cheech and Chong living together again, looking forward to the upcoming Rolling Stones concert. Chong is given the task of picking up the tickets; however, he ends up selling them for a bag of weed and the boys are forced to sneak into the concert disguised as roadies. They dress like roadies and get into the concert by carrying chairs so they can watch from backstage. They accidentally drop instruments as they try to help set up the stage, so they are charged with sitting onstage while holding water bottles for the stars. Nobody wants that job, because it is too demeaning. After the concert, the boys try to escape into the crowd but are caught and forced to load up the vans. Since they keep dropping expensive guitars, they are made to drive Mick and the rest of the band around. When they get lost and cause the Stones to miss a gig, the audience thinks they will get fired, but they inadvertently save Mick from being kidnapped. They are rewarded by being allowed to appear onstage with the Stones.

I do remember setting the second story in Canada's cold, snowy frontier, but they didn't like it, and I don't recall the third story at all. It was long ago and, in any case, we never shot either of the two stories from which they picked that night. That's when I decided to start writing *Nice Dreams*.

CHAPTER FIFTEEN

NICE DREAMS

Los Angeles, California, 1980

I wrote the first draft of *Nice Dreams* with a stoner friend of mine from Vancouver. Michael Malcolm had been married to Shelby's sister for some time and we became good friends because of our mutual love for the magic herb. Mike was and still is involved in Vancouver's hippie artist community since the sixties. I spent quite some time at Mike's studio smoking the herb and chatting about the movie. I wrote most of it in Vancouver and came down to Los Angeles when it was time for preproduction. I brought Mike with me and intended to have him help with the writing as we shot the movie; however, Cheech did not appreciate the fact that I was writing the movie without his involvement and he didn't want Mike around. In fact, he told him to fuck off at one point. I was shocked at Cheech's rude remark, but we had a movie to shoot, so I never called him on it. And Mike was very cool about it so we just pretended it never happened.

I wanted this movie to be an easy ride for both of us; I set it in Los Angeles and Malibu, so Cheech and I would not have to travel far. Cheech and his wife, Rikki, were in the process of adopting their first little daughter and needed time at home, so it worked out well for everyone. Shelby had given birth to our youngest son Gilbran while we were in Vancouver, so the Cheech and Chong houses were babyland during that time.

The title, *Nice Dreams,* evolved from a drawing of Mike's; he had been designing ice-cream trucks. I noticed that the sign ICE CREAMS could be changed to "Nice Dreams" without much effort, and since the story had us selling pot from an ice-cream truck, it was perfect. We also had Stacy Keach and a couple of his friends playing cops, only this time I made Stacy's character, Stadenko, much darker and perverted. I brought back Pee-wee Herman as the hamburger man from the nuthouse. We also introduced Sandra Bernhard to the world as one of the nuts from the mental home we called Casa del Wacko.

Cheech and I wrote and performed all the bits on the albums together, but the movie scripts were different. I ended up being the guy who wrote the scenarios down on paper. I wrote *Up in Smoke* with Cheech and his cousin Louie. However, I was the guy who put the script on paper, and I was the guy who crafted the tone and direction of the movie. I also wrote the title track "Up in Smoke." I wrote the song alone deliberately to show Lou Adler and Cheech that I write alone. When Cheech heard my version of the song he wrote a Spanish version that you hear in the movie, but he used my melody. Cheech still insists to this day that I did not write the movies. (He also insists that I did not write my book *The I Chong.* When he told me that I had to smile because he prefaced the remark by telling me that *The I Chong* was the worst book he had ever read and it got the worst reviews.) The only reason I wrote those movies was because I had to—no one else was going to write them. And that is also the reason I directed them—no one else wanted the job. I loved writing Cheech and Chong movies, and I especially loved the power trip of directing them. It was such a sweet feeling to know that if I wanted a fake swimming pool screen over a grow room I would get it, no questions asked.

Howard had even gotten in with the head of production

at Paramount, Don Simpson, who was a big fan. Don sent us a letter of congratulations for *Next Movie,* and Howard, never one to miss an opportunity, hit Don up for a suite of offices so we could work on a project for Paramount. We got the suite and a secretary, who came in every day and sat and knitted and read books because we never used the place. I visited a few times, but we already had offices at Universal and Columbia with movies set up at both studios. There just wasn't enough of me to go around. But when I think of the deals Howard Brown got for us back then, I marvel at the genius of that man. Unfortunately, while he got us work, he also helped to tear Cheech and me apart.

The split between Cheech and me started the day I brought Shelby in to play a pretty young woman who was working out at a World Gym where my character was doing business with the manager. While he and I are chatting, Cheech wanders around, staring at the girls in the gym as they work out. Cheech decides to try a couple of bench presses. As he picks the weight off the rack, Shelby screams and Cheech loses control of the barbell and is trapped with the weight pressing against his throat. Alerted by the scream, the entire gym rushes to Shelby's aid, totally ignoring the guy (Cheech) who really needs help. I wander over to Cheech and pull the weight off his throat, but before he can say a word I let go of the weight and yell, "Push it—come on, man, you can do it." Cheech's expressions sell the misery and pain I am causing him and we all laughed hard when we looked at the dailies that night. All the dailies looked good, but that particular bit brought down the house. Right in the middle of the laughs Cheech comes over to me and whispers, "That was the weakest shit ever, man."

When he said it, I turned and looked into his eyes to see if he was serious. And he was deadly serious! Everyone loved the bit! It was so funny it hardly needed editing—the editors even used it in the trailer. And it really showcased Cheech's comic ability because the weights were phony, yet he sold them. *Weakest shit ever? Was he serious?*

This surprised me because I had never seen that side of Cheech before. His eyes were blazing with hate. He hated being laughed at. This is a serious problem, especially if you make a living being a comedian. The question was whether he hated the bit or hated the fact that Shelby was the one who caused the pain. I had a strong feeling he did not want Shelby to be in the movie, mainly because Shelby has influence over me as any beautiful wife would have over her husband. However, I made it clear to Cheech that as the director I had the right to pursue my vision and I could cast anyone I want. Yeah, I could have used another actress. Casting one's wife in a movie is unacceptable in certain macho circles, but I did not run in those circles. I owed this to Shelby. She stood by without complaint as I cast Rikki in *Next Movie*. And I did that purposely so no one could say I favored my wife over his.

But Cheech saw the writing on the wall, long before I knew it was there. He knew that Shelby would one day replace him as my partner. I never envisioned that scenario, not in my wildest dreams. I felt that Cheech and I would be together forever. I mean, why not? We had the perfect gig: getting high, then talking about getting high. I don't know about Cheech, but I felt that it took very little effort to be a Cheech or a Chong—no effort at all really. Get high, be funny, and try to make people laugh, that was all we had to do. Oh, yeah, and make records, movies, videos, and shitloads of money. This is what we called work.

Rikki let me in on another reason for Cheech's sudden dark moods. He is a very talented, complex man, and like so many comedians before him, Cheech was not satisfied being known as the "funny guy." He wanted to be taken seriously, which is why he showed America his serious side in movies like *Tin Cup* and television shows like *Nash Bridges*. He had hateful, jealous moods that changed the funny cheerful guy into someone entirely different. My first encounter with this darker Cheech was that night in the screening room watching dailies. The only time I had seen something similar to that dark side was when we were writing the show for the Redd Foxx Club and I drew a little lightbulb at the top of the set list indicating a brilliant idea. Cheech looked at my drawing and said, "Why can't I do that?" I thought he was making a joke at first and then I saw the frustration in his eyes. Cheech was frustrated that he couldn't sketch a little drawing like that. Cheech loved art and artistic people but he never had any love for his own creations, except for his pottery, where he excelled. He had become a very accomplished potter during his time in Canada and had he kept it up there may have been Cheech pottery in all the museums in the world. He was that good. But sometimes knowing what other artists create can intimidate one to the point of frustration. It is the same with writing. Being a writer is the most honest job on the planet. We write because it is soothing, fun, exciting, and fulfilling, though it can also be a terrible chore that we put off until we hate ourselves for being so critical and judgmental. Procrastination is a state of suspended situations. It was fun writing Cheech and Chong bits. And Cheech loved writing the bits, too, only, as Cheech told me, he writes in his head. This is how we wrote when we were together. In other words, he would take what I wrote and make it his own when we performed the bit. This is why we were so successful. The combination worked.

In addition to writing, I know the reason I could direct our movie was because I was never educated in the school system. My education came from the street, where you have to be real with whatever you do if you expect to make it. Most public schools, in my humble opinion, are concerned with good grades and memory skills, which is fine for some fields. However, in the creative field, such as writing, art, or comedy, structure can actually hinder the creative process. When students compare their artistic attempts with a master's work they've memorized, some of them experience frustration and inadequacy while others are inspired and motivated to create their own artistic expression. One approach is more studied, and the other is more instinctual. "Judge not and ye shall not be judged" is the creed to which a writer or director should adhere. When you look at something without judging it, you tend to see the whole picture and not a limited one. This is another reason I make a good director. Rather than judging dailies I just enjoyed them like a regular audience member and I used them to continue writing the film. I'm not the one who does the work anyway. It's the Muse, the Father, the Presence that goeth before me.

But getting back to the movie . . . .

The nuthouse scene in *Nice Dreams* to me underscored the insanity of the so-called drug world. America is obsessed with drugs. The television industry is run almost entirely on ads from drug companies that, in my opinion, are actually inventing diseases, as if we didn't already have enough real ones to cope with. Casa del Wacko, the nuthouse in *Nice Dreams,* was taken from a real halfway house for wealthy people with mental problems. It was located in a motel on Chuanga between Hollywood and North Hollywood. My buddy Tony Vascaria was institutionalized there during one of his stints for drug possession and use. This is the way of the government, folks. They take a man with a history of drug problems and send him to a mental hospital. His job? Dispensing drugs to mentally ill people.

By this time, Tony had fallen back into the world of heroin pretty seriously. I tried to use Tony as a sort of road manager when Cheech and I were touring. Needless to say, it did not work out as well as it could have. I wanted to employ the guy, but a junkie can be a placement challenge even for a stoner like myself. But I slept on the problem and bingo! Solved. I hired Tony as a writer.

"A writer? Hey, I can't write, man."

"Sure you can, Tony. You write funny shit all the time."

"No, I say funny shit. I don't write anything."

"Well, then say the funny shit."

"What do you mean?"

"Just say the funny shit into a tape recorder and we will have the secretary type it up."

"Yeah, I can do that."

And so this is how Tony became a writer. I bought him a tape recorder, the way Lou Adler did for Cheech and me when we first started out. And Tony used it faithfully. I got him a salary of a couple of hundred dollars a week, and right as the money ran out, so did Tony.

Tony died of complications from the effects of prolonged drug use. I received news of his death directly from the ambulance driver, who, after telling me of Tony's demise, wanted to know who was responsible for the ambulance bill. I hung up the phone while the guy was waiting for me to give him an address and I stared out the window. Tony had died. I began to laugh at the way the ambulance driver tried to get me to pay for the call. This was something Tony would have remembered and used as a bit.

Tony's funeral was held a couple of weeks later and the old comics came to pay their respects, along with Tony's ex-wives, girlfriends, and dope friends. They all wore sunglasses and huddled together as if they were a sports team. In some respects they were a team; they were the loves and associates of this man with a sharp sense of humor. Even in the darkest moments of his drug addiction, he would suddenly laugh out loud at some vision that cracked him up.

Jackie Gayle, the great Vegas comic and a close friend of Tony's and Sally's, said the funniest line when we were carrying the casket to the burial site. The site was on the side of a hill, and we had to struggle uphill with the casket, prompting Jackie to exclaim in a loud voice, "You fucking Mexican, why couldn't you spring for a level piece of land? You cheap bastard." We all started laughing and almost dropped the body of our dear friend.

Tony's death was inevitable given all the drugs he abused. Sticking a needle in your arm and pumping heroin into your system really is death itself when you consider it. A heroin high is a total absence of feeling, so I have been told. I have never experienced the high but I have seen the results too many times.

Tony had not been able to secure us anything more than a few freebies and was heavy into junk. Tony even brought me a packet of brown heroin when I asked him about Lenny's habit. I wanted to know whether it made him funnier. "Did it make him more creative?" I would ask. Tony would reply, "Try it and see for yourself."

I kept the heroin hidden in my drawer while we were at the cabin but in the end I flushed it down the toilet. I had seen too many hopeless junkies and I know they all started with their first snort. That was a test for me and I passed it.

CHAPTER SIXTEEN

THINGS ARE TOUGH ALL OVER

Chicago, Illinois, 1980

Things Are Tough All Over was the third and last movie in the Howard Brown deal, and the second we did for Columbia. They were happy because *Nice Dreams* did so well. This third movie was supposed to be called *Riding High*, a story about the Peter Principle and Mick Jagger and the Stones. Cheech did not want to be left out of the loop as he was in *Nice Dreams*. So he went on strike. He refused to work on *Riding High*. He wanted to at least have a say in what the movie was about and what to call it, so he started writing his own script. Howard and I finally had to sit down and discuss our next move, which was to give him what he wanted. So we did.

Cheech told me his idea for the movie. He wanted to do something about the Arab oil embargo. In 1980, the Arab states had limited the supply of oil to the United States to raise the price of oil. Sound familiar? So oil, Arabs, and what else? Cheech couldn't think of anything else, so I started adding what I wanted to see. Dope, of course!

Howard was upset that I was no longer the director and he expressed concern because we had sold the studios on my ability to deliver, and the first two pictures showed them that I was

doing the job right. He was worried that our editor, Tom Avildsen, who would now direct, would not be able to deliver. So I
explained to Howard that I was still the director. Tom would
direct from an editor's point of view and I would do what I always did: get something funny on the screen. I really loved the
arrangement because I didn't have to do anything except concentrate on my character. That is what I assumed would happen
and, for the most part, it did. I still made decisions and wrote
scenes and struggled with the thin plot. There was no plot, actually: just a couple of numbskulls trying to deliver a car full of
dope, while two evil Arab dope dealers try to kill them for mess-
ing around with their girlfriends. The girlfriends, or the Fifis as
they were called in the film, were played by none other than our
very own wives, Shelby and Rikki.

We started the shoot in Chicago, drove across country, and
ended up in Vegas. The Chicago shoot was hell because of the
cold. "The coldest day in history" read the newspaper headlines.
It was one hundred degrees below zero with the windchill factor. And there we were, shooting in a car wash—walking with
our heads down, like the blind leading the blind. Or rather the
stoned leading the stoned! The cold was so intense that you
could not expose any part of your bare skin to it. Cheech and
Chong inadvertently get stuck in a convertible and ride through
with the top down. They get stuck because they are very stupid
guys, which endears them to the audience. And I loved playing
my character. It was so much fun being high and stupid at the
same time. It made our lives fun and exciting and rich. We had
it made in the shade. We got to live out our fantasy lives as
these characters.

We formed a band for *Things Are Tough* and this is where I
now feel we made our first mistake. Gaye Delorme, the fantastic guitarist who cowrote "Earache My Eye," put the band to-

gether under my supervision. We were supposed to be a very bad cover band who never learned the proper lyrics for the songs we covered. But the musicians were very good studio musicians and you cannot fake bad music, not with musicians who have spent many hours working on their craft.

Our only gig was at an empty dance hall in Chicago, where we meet club owners and bad guys Habib and Abdul (played by Cheech and Chong). The music upsets Habib so much he decides to banish Cheech and Chong from town. They are instructed to deliver a car full of coke to their connections in Vegas. We go from the coldest day on record to the sweltering heat of the Nevada desert. Cheech and Chong take peyote, a powerful mind-expander found growing in cow shit, and spend a good part of the movie stumbling around in the desert.

My favorite scene is where Cheech and Chong sit around playing guitar and singing while waiting to be rescued. As Cheech sings a tune called "Me and My Old Lady" written by Gaye Delorme, a parade of vehicles stops to listen to the song. But the boys are too engrossed in what they are doing to even see the would-be rescuers. Their angel appears in the form of a nutcase Vegas comic named Rip Taylor. He is a little on the gay side and dresses his new friends up in women's clothing, so we do a huge part of the movie in drag. Cheech told me he liked wearing women's clothes, especially in the hot desert. I think he liked the women's clothes for a different reason, but that's my personal opinion. Hey, I like dressing up in women's clothes myself. I think its kinda sexy in a kinky sort of way and your balls are not cramped up like they are in jeans.

Vegas was the best part of the shoot; we had the most fun living and working there. It's a perfect place to shoot a movie because it never closes. No matter how long of a day we put in shooting, the city was always open. The casinos were happening 24/7 and the showrooms welcomed the movie crew and their money like old friends.

I sent for my mom and dad while we were there because Mom's health was failing and I knew it was now or never. They had the best time staying in suites, with twenty-four-hour room service and all the shows at their disposal. We took them to see Liza Minnelli and got the best seats in the place. Halfway through the show Liberace came and sat with us, causing a commotion with my parents. Pop handed me his program and asked me to get Liberace's autograph. I had to calm Pop down a little because he was so excited. Of course he was. This was Liberace! This was Mom and Pop's Elvis! This is who they swooned over.

I remember when Liberace did his television show and watching the look of joy on my parents' faces. Mom and Pop stared at Lee the entire show, and when we were escorted backstage to Liza's dressing room they were given the ultimate thrill—having their pictures taken with both Liberace and Liza. My parents went back to Qualicum Beach after Vegas and showed the picture to all their friends and relatives in the little beach town on Vancouver Island.

I watched the look of pure worship as they took in every word Liberace said to them. They were enthralled and I could see that Liberace was enjoying the attention. Lee was not alone. He had his boyfriend with him, hovering around the great man like a secret service agent.

The striking thing about Liberace was that his flamboyance was just an act. Yet he had been in the limelight for so many years that his celebrated gayness was part and parcel of who he was. Back in the heyday of the fifties, Liberace was one of perhaps five people who could sell out Madison Square Garden at a moment's notice. America loved this gentle soul because he was so polite and kind to his mother, who made the genius practice the piano for hours on end. Liberace was much bigger than his legend. His obvious gayness was his strength as long as he didn't confirm his homosexuality. As far as people were concerned, Liberace was a classically trained piano player who loved to be flamboyant. This image pandered to the millions of Americans who would rather be kept in the dark about people they put on pedestals, as opposed to someone like, say, Lenny Bruce, who would burst this bubble of comfortable ignorance every chance he got.

Liberace never denied his homosexuality during his lifetime. He always had a male companion or valet, who traveled with him wherever he went. He was never married, unlike closeted homosexuals like Rock Hudson, who had to protect their leading man images. No, Liberace was who he was. He was gay and he never ran away from that image. He embraced it and it made him a very popular and wealthy entertainer. It was a thrill meeting him, especially when he fawned over my parents the way he did.

Liza was also wonderful and kind to us that night. I remember her sharing a Peter Sellers story with us. When I mentioned Peter was a good friend of mine, she grabbed me and told me how Peter insisted she bring her Oscar to bed with them. Liza had, of course, won an Academy Award for her performance in *Cabaret* and this excited Peter Sellers to no end. She and Peter had their fling and she, along with the hundreds of other women in Peter's life, still loved and cared deeply for the comic genius.

Cheech and I enjoyed making *Things Are Tough* because we were in our element—stars of our own movie, playing characters we invented, and doing all the dope jokes we could write. This was heaven as far as I was concerned.

The other perk of our movie career was that we did not have to live in the United States to make our movies. We could live anywhere, like the South of France. Shelby and her sister, Forrest, moved to Paris when we shot *Up in Smoke.* Shelby had been studying French and wanted to live in France so she would get the entire experience. So while I was away shooting *Smoke,* she and her sister moved to Paris with their two little boys, Paris and Mylo. They stayed in a one-room apartment on the Left Bank and had their meals in a little Vietnamese restaurant nearby. They shopped and lived "French" for months until I finally told her to come home.

The movie was over and we were on a Canadian tour so we met in Regina Sask. It had been months since I had seen my love, so when I crawled into bed after the gig I noticed she had put on a few pounds. The steady diet of French food had taken her skinny little girl's body and replaced it with a "va va voom, oh my god, this feels so sexy" body. I was more than thrilled to be cuddled next to my love goddess once again. And I do believe she got pregnant soon after her return.

Shelby's French skills were utilized in *Things Are Tough All Over* when she played the French love interest of the Arab bad guys. One of the funniest scenes in the history of Cheech and Chong movies was the herpes scene where a "hair technician" is placing a wig on Habib's head, and Habib starts talking about his old hairpiece, only he pronounces it with his Arab accent making the word sound like herpes.

"You have herpes?" asks the terrified hair stylist.

"Oh, yes, I have herpes [hairpiece] for many years," replies Habib. "Yes, many years! No one knew. I never told anyone. It is embarrassing when you have herpes [hairpiece]. Do you have herpes [hairpiece]?" Habib asks the hair stylist.

"No," replies the hair stylist, who thinks Habib is disgusting with his talk about herpes.

"Then I give you my herpes! I insist you take my old herpes." The play on accents and words were always a huge part of the Cheech and Chong experience.

Things Are Tough All Over was released to the Cheech and Chong audiences in 1982 and it sort of stayed under the radar. It was enjoyed, but it didn't create the kind of attention that the other three had. I think playing two roles did not help the film because the stars, Cheech and Chong, disappear for too long a stretch. Their characters are the stars and the other characters they play are really supporting actors. So the imbalance messes with the reality we were trying to create as we had in the previous films.

When you disappear into a character, you essentially disappear. If you are a good actor you vanish as one character and someone else appears. This is why Bob Hope and Bing Crosby were bad actors. Because whatever character they played, they were always "Hope and Crosby." They never disappeared into another character. Not that they were unable to. On the contrary, Bing Crosby won an Academy Award for his acting in a serious movie. Bob Hope could also act and did so in a couple of movies like *Bachelor in Paradise* and *The Facts of Life*. But to make a comedic movie work, you have to stay in character. When the movie wrapped, we decided to move to the South of France: Cannes, the queen of the film festival world, the playground of the rich and famous. Ah, yes, and the French franc in 1981. The American dollar ruled! We were the best in the world! Everyone wanted our American dollars. The French franc went as low as eleven francs for one dollar. It might have gone down as low as eight francs to a dollar but it hovered around fourteen francs for the longest while. The strong dollar made living abroad so sensible. You could live like a king for next to nothing. This was, of course, pre-9/11. Travel was so different compared with today's security checks, long lines of frightened travelers checking to see if they might have forgotten some dangerous item such as a nail file, or makeup, or water bottles. In 1981, they encouraged passengers to visit the cockpit and help fly the plane, and some did so while holding a glass of champagne. The airplanes had smoking sections where one could light up a cigarette or a cigar. And this was after a real four-course dinner.

Oh, yes, the world before 9/11 was a world that will never be again. I consider myself so blessed having lived during the time when America was hailed as the number one country on the planet. When travel was a luxury and not a military exercise. Going through the checkpoints at airports now is akin to entering a Communist country during the Cold War. And we had no idea how wonderful life was back then. No idea! We just took every precious bit of freedom for granted, *entirely* for granted. And this is the result. What goes around comes around. Yin and yang. Cheech and Chong.

After *Things Are Tough All Over*, we took a break from the grind. Cheech reacquainted himself with the Malibu Beach crowd while Rikki worked on becoming a world-class equestrian. Cheech, in turn, was becoming a world-class horse schlepper, helping Rikki load the horses into trailers and rubbing them down after a hard workout. And he was beginning to hate his life as a horse wrangler. He missed being on the road where we were the most important people in the room. He didn't miss the work as much as he missed being the important one. And when he was Cheech of Cheech and Chong he was the important one. He was the funniest, cutest, and craziest, while I played the straight, fucked-up stoner. It is very tough going from getting ovations to standing in the rain trying to load a thoroughbred horse into a trailer.

The horse people who Rikki associated with had no idea who Cheech and Chong were, so Cheech was treated like a "Mexican" at some of the functions they attended. The abuse started to wear on Cheech and made him feel bitter and angry. Rikki, who was so wrapped up with her equestrian career, did not see the source of his anger.

Meanwhile, Shelby, the kids, and I had rented a house in a little town outside of Cannes called Taoule. Shelby and Forrest had checked out the place before we moved and found schools for the kids. Our time in Cannes was quite spectacular in many ways. We always ate in the quaint little mom-and-pop restaurants, the ones where you don't need a menu because there are only a few really good dishes. And no matter how many times you eat there, they still treat you like foreigners who are learning the language. The locals consider anyone who doesn't speak their certain dialect a tourist. It is a kind of European dissing that has gone on since the beginning of France. Food in the South of France is like a religion to those who live there. You learn to worship food to the extent that the chef becomes the high priest and you must bow down to the master whenever you have the chance.

Shelby's parents, Edna and Harry, came to visit us and we took them to our favorite little restaurant. It was Sunday night and the restaurant was packed with locals. We stuck out like sore thumbs, especially Harry, poster boy for the rugged Canadian, who was in France for the first time. He was big, 6'1", and had made a living on the docks as a longshoreman. Harry was raised on a farm in Saskatchewan and had developed a drinking problem during his time on the docks. Harry was a man's

man, drunk or sober. The toughest men on the docks respected
and feared Harry because they saw firsthand how strong and
tough he could be if riled up. Like many alcoholics, Harry could
be a lamb or a tornado and people who knew him tiptoed
around him when he was drunk so as not to awaken the dangerous side of him.

That night in the restaurant a French couple sitting at the
table next to us was getting a huge charge out of the way Shelby
and Forrest were speaking French. The waitress spoke no English whatsoever and her French was the local dialect, so she had
to ask the girls to repeat their requests over and over, much to
the delight of the couple sitting next to us. I watched and was
getting a little pissed at the very rude manner in which they
were laughing at our clumsy attempts to communicate in
French. The girls didn't notice so they continued to speak their
rudimentary French while the rude couple laughed at every
mangled phrase.

Harry ordered a roast half chicken because it was the only
thing on the menu he recognized, and when his meal arrived,
Harry just studied his chicken, planning on how he was going
to eat the thing. The French couple were screaming with laughter at Harry's crude attempt to cut the chicken. I was about to
call them out on their rude behavior when Harry's knife sliced
through the center of the chicken, spraying the couple with a
mixture of wine sauce and chicken juice. Harry muttered a very
soft apology and kept on eating. This time I was the one laughing hard at the stunned expression on the French guy's face, as
he wiped the juice from his jacket and shirt. The girl had chicken
juice splattered on her glasses and she was close to tears as the
two of them gathered their belongings and hustled out of the
restaurant in a huff.

Cheech came to visit a couple of times while we were in

France. The first time was when we were in Arcachon on the Atlantic Coast. Shelby's French teacher from Los Angeles had recommended this little fishing village famous for its bouillabaisse, a traditional Provençal fish stew, and its fresh baked buns. We were in our element at the beach. This was the reason I wanted to live in Vancouver and then in Los Angeles. I was totally committed to the beach scene wherever it was. My father, who was born in Vancouver, told me about the days when he and his family used to catch crab and pick oysters right off the beaches. I would sit huddled next to the wood-burning kitchen stove in our little bungalow in Calgary in the middle of winter, listening to these stories and imagining what it would be like to live right on the beach. And lo and behold, here we were living the dream. When Cheech and Rikki arrived, it was hot and the beaches were crowded, but they insisted on going to a nude beach. I argued against it, but of course, no one listened to me. When we drove up to the parking area I was amazed at the size of the crowd. There had to be at least a thousand people, all totally nude. Walking, sitting, splashing in the water, standing in line at the snack area, all totally naked. There were mostly young, healthy, very sexy women. There might have been men there as well but I only saw the women. French women with the tightest, sexiest bodies, all tanned to perfection. The force of the naked beauties created an atmosphere of hightened awareness of the beauty of the human species. We found a place to lay out our blanket that was fairly close to the snack bar. I had to go into the water immediately and submerge to hide my growing erection. Cheech went in for the instant deboner cooling-off period, too. I noticed there were a quite a few men in the water probably for the same reason. It was sensory overload. Everywhere you looked, you could see beautiful women. The cold Atlantic Ocean kept the steaming hot erections under control until I became used to the sights. The trick, not surprisingly, was to look at the ones who would not arouse the sleeping giant. It took discipline, but eventually I could even stroll to the snack bar without having to jump back into the water.

That night we dined at a restaurant suggested by Shelby's French teacher. Located a little way from the tourist cafés on the beach, this café's specialty was, of course, bouillabaisse served with homemade, fresh baked dinner buns. The first course was what we in America would consider a meal and I was about to ask for the check when the main course arrived. The chef, the waiter, and the manager carried a tub filled with every type of seafood imaginable and placed it carefully in the center of the table. It was without a doubt the finest, most satisfying meal I had ever had up to that point in my life. You need to have a local make reservations for you to get into these fine dining restaurants, where the chef spends the entire day preparing a meal for people who love and understand food, much like art galleries attract art lovers—collectors who know what they are looking at. The French appreciate the finer things in life, and to be a part of that culture was an experience I will always cherish.

Cheech enjoyed the experience as well; however, he was a Malibu guy to the bone. As much as he enjoyed the naked French girls, he belonged in Malibu, where he owned a piece of the beach. It was his home and refuge. This is where he ruled, where he attended countless parties, smoked the best dope, and drank the finest beer. Times were loose in the early eighties. Mel Gibson would never have been arrested back then. The Malibu cops would have most likely driven his drunk ass home, with a deputy driving his vehicle so he would have his ride when he sobered up. Cheech experienced that lenient attitude more than a few times.

One time, Cheech was speeding home in his Porsche smoking a big fatty when he zoomed past the cops, who had set up a speed trap. Unaware of the cops behind him, Cheech flicked the roach out of the window. The burning doob hit the ground and exploded in a shower of sparks. The police followed Cheech for almost a mile before Cheech realized he was being pulled over.

As he sat and waited for the cops, he realized he did not have his ID with him. He had left his wallet on the dresser when he slipped on a pair of shorts after his daily body surfing session. *OK, the papers for the Porsche ... where the hell are they? Why am I stopped here? Oh yeah, I just got pulled over. OK, just act cool. You are not drunk. Just a little stoned.*

"My license? Uh, isn't it on the bumper?"

The cop looked at Cheech for what seemed like forever, and then realized Cheech was famous.

"Hey, Cheech! We thought it was you! How's it going? Loved the movies, man. Where's Chong? Hey, was that real dope in *Up in Smoke?* Ease off the gas pedal, OK? You were tripping pretty hard there for a while. And don't throw the roaches out of the car 'cause this is a fire area. Say hi to Chong for me, OK? Take care, buddy!"

Cheech never had a chance to answer, thanks to the killer bud he had just inhaled about a half hour before. His mouth was so dry he couldn't have answered if he wanted to. *Speeding? Was I speeding? Where am I going? Oh, yeah, home! Did I just get stopped by the cops?*

The cops followed Cheech until he turned into his driveway, making sure their favorite comedian got home safely. This was Malibu during the late seventies. Thirty years later, Mel Gibson, who was in a "Malibu state of mind" or, in other words, "pissy-eyed drunk," was arrested and booked for DUI. The

"King of Malibu" was so drunk that he turned a routine traffic stop into a blistering attack on the Jews of the world. The Malibu police tried to give Mel the same treatment they gave Cheech years before, but Mel would not keep his big mouth shut. Excessive alcohol takes out the brain and turns people into blithering idiots.

Pot, on the other hand, tends to make the user more aware of his surroundings. I know from personal experience that pot makes you drive carefully, sometimes a little too carefully. But too careful is a good way to drive. Alcohol kills. Drunk drivers kill thousands of people every year, and the cops know this because they are the ones who have to clean up the mess. They know this and yet it is the pot smokers who fill the jails of America. Mel was still drunk when they let him go, yet they put Paris Hilton in jail for forty-five days simply because she was late for a court appearance. It doesn't take a rocket scientist to guess which judge drinks and which judge smokes pot.

People always ask me if I think we could make the movies like *Up in Smoke* today. And I tell them no. I was incarcerated for nine months simply because I made those movies back in the seventies and the eighties. It is in the court records. I was incarcerated for nine months for taking responsibility for a box of glass water pipes that was shipped across state lines! The Republician Party with the Axis of Evil—Bush, Cheney, and Rove—has systematically torn the Constitution of the United States of America to shreds in the past seven years they have been in power. But enough about those idiots. Let's get back to the Cheech and Chong story.

While Cheech was hitting the party scene in Malibu, I was working on scripts in France and toying with the idea of doing a Cheech and Chong film festival in the fall of 1981. I know that was the date because I had Ed Ruscha, the number one selling artist in America, do the poster. I had never been to a film festival before, but living in Cannes gave me reason to believe that it couldn't be that difficult. Hey, I had just finished writing and directing three major motion pictures, how hard could a film festival be. I had hooked up with, let me call him Stuart, a young mover and groover from Amsterdam, and he assured me he had the connections that would make it all happen.

Paramount, in the meantime, had offered us a million dollars to do a live concert movie. Eddie Murphy had done a couple and was making millions from them, so it seemed like an easy thing to do. The problem with me is I never take the easy way. Why? I guess it's because I have always found that if you wanted something bad enough you have to do it yourself, get your hands dirty. This is why I directed the movies. I could not trust my vision with someone else. Because it was my vision and only I knew how it was supposed to go.

I flew back to Los Angeles to meet with the honchos over at Paramount to talk about the live concert taping, and on the flight over I had a great idea. Why not take the million and do a movie about us doing a live performance concert?

Of course, when I ran my idea past Cheech he immediately said no. He did not want to do it. He was dead-set against my "Chong way" of taking projects and doing them differently from what was proposed. But I knew I was right. A concert movie about two guys going to a film festival and performing their act to adoring fans. Amsterdam is the pot capital of the universe and Cheech and Chong are gods over there. They have smoke shops named after our movies. The Queen of the Netherlands, Queen Beatrice, used to grab a girlfriend and go incognito to our flicks, so a movie about the whole pot experience in Amsterdam would be the natural way to go.

Cheech did not see it my way, so I had to put up forty-five

thousand dollars of my own money to get things rolling. As soon as Paramount saw that I was serious, they arranged for me to get the necessary budget to make it happen. When that happened, Cheech came onboard. He not only came onboard, but also proceeded to write some of the funniest shit I have ever seen on the big screen. The E.T. bit where he played an alien named Eddie Torres, the extra testicle, still makes me laugh no matter how many times I've seen it.

Paramount wanted to name the movie *Still Smokin,* so we had to go to Lou Adler to get the proper permission. I was a little apprehensive because we weren't on good terms, but he came around. I woke up the next morning and decided to drive my Rolls Corniche convertible from Cannes to Amsterdam alone to get things rolling. Shelby was very supportive and was actually glad to get me out of her hair for a while. She wasn't used to me being around 24/7 and we were getting on each other's nerves. We had never really been together that much before and the closeness was wearing her down. I liked not being on the road for a change but I had to admit I was getting pretty bored living in paradise—where every day was sunny and perfect and every meal was a gourmet delight, where the wine was excellent and so reasonably priced, where the tomatoes tasted so fresh and full of flavor and the bread was always freshly baked. The problems with this perfect life began emerging at mealtime when we started by ordering wine by the glass. Then by the bottle. And then two bottles. We were so much in love when it was by the glass. Still friends with one bottle. But by the time we had graduated to two bottles, we were fighting, arguing, and calling each other nasty names while still in the restaurant.

I had also run out of things to do in Cannes. I had my gym where I worked out daily and I had the little cafés where I would sit and write, but I was ready to travel somewhere. Anywhere. So it was off to Amsterdam. I needed to get going. This retirement shit was killing my soul.

Shelby kissed me good-bye and bounced happily back to the rented house while I pulled away in my big, shiny, black Rolls convertible. My first stop after driving for an hour was at the gas station, where I encountered my first obstacle: the gas tank opening was too small for the European hose to fit. Damn! I also found that many of the filling stations did not take credit cards, and fuck me, that's all I ever carried. I had all the cards but very little cash. And to my utter dismay, everyone dealt in cash between Cannes and Amsterdam.

I finally solved the gas tank problem by creating a funnel using a plastic water bottle carved to fit into the gas tank. And I drove to a four-star hotel in Nice and took care of the cash problem, thanks to the good old American Express card. Don't leave home without it! So with some cash and a full gas tank I was good to explore France. I put the top down and took as many side roads as I could find, staying away from the freeways. I stopped at the most out of the way places whenever I had the urge and I had the urge quite often.

I drove past an abandoned castle that looked interesting. The walled estate was on the corner of a field and totally exposed to the elements. Trees were growing out of the walls and through the roof of the main castle. The underbrush had almost obliterated the walkways, but you could still make out the different structures: animal enclosures, barns, and grain silos. I sat in the car and observed the grounds. The old castle had a mystic quality about it, as if ghosts were hovering about like dragonflies staking out their territory.

I drove on and soon I was near the France–Belgium border where signs of war were evident on some of the buildings. You could see bullet holes and possibly tank rounds in the walls of the buildings. I visualized the armies of old marching toward the front, passing wounded stragglers making their way back to the field hospitals and safety. Old World War II pictures came to my mind, as I drove on the same roads where legions of Roman soldiers had marched and then years later, trucks had been driven first by French loyalists and then by the hated Nazi storm troopers.

I stopped in Belgium and spent the evening wandering around the town square listening to classical music and looking for the right restaurant. The place was packed with tourists enjoying the summer night. As I wandered alone down ancient cobblestone streets, I could feel ghosts of the buildings watching me as I looked at the windows and tried to imagine what it was like two hundred or five hundred years ago. *Have I been here before in another life?* I thought. *Is that what made me stop at this particular place? Or is this my very first time here? I can't seem to remember. Well, I best get some sleep and get ready for Amsterdam.*

I was looking forward to Amsterdam for the most obvious reason. Legalized pot! A place where you can relax and enjoy a pipe without getting bummed out by the cops. I heard many things about Amsterdam through *High Times* magazine, which holds an annual event called the Cannabis Cup. This is a weeklong event where growers from all over the world compete for the best bud award. I was eager to taste some bud, as things were pretty dry in Cannes. I did score some pretty decent bud in Arcachon from a dealer who was waiting to go to jail. He had been busted and sentenced, but the jails were full and he was put on a waiting list. And of course, while he was waiting he was still doing the very thing that sentenced him to jail in the first place. What crazy insane laws. Well, Amsterdam seems to have the drug problem under control because they have licensed coffee bars that deal in pot, hash, and mushrooms.

I called Stuart the minute I arrived and was taken out on the town for an evening of sampling all the local delights with him and a couple of his friends. The first pot bar featured some buds from Africa. The owners of the bar greeted me with a pipe stuffed with the fine African weed. I took my usual little tiny toke and handed the pipe to the guy next to me. The gang looked at me like I was crazy. "That's it? One little toke and you give up the pipe? Hey, where is the Chong from *Up in Smoke*? You know, the guy who hands Cheech the giant joint?"

The pot hit me hard. I felt dizzy and had to sit down immediately. That was not normal pot. There was something in it. I started feeling paranoid. *What was in that shit?* I tried to talk but nothing came out. My mouth and throat were completely dry, and before I could say anything, I was handed a glass of what I thought was water. It was something else that I had never tasted before. *Fuck, now what did I just take?* The liquid lubricated my vocal cords enough to tell my hosts that I was feeling sick and had to go home. My Dutch hosts loaded me into a vehicle and drove me back to the hotel. When I got to my room, I told the guys carrying me that I could take it from there. They insisted on opening the door to my room and then, with promises to see me later, the guys went back to their party. I passed out soon after they closed the door to my room. I woke up face-down on the rug a few feet from the bed eight hours later!

I stayed close to the hotel the rest of the day, walking and taking in the sights. The weather was cold and rainy, but the vibe of the place was mellow and laid back: people walked, rode bicycles, hopped on and off streetcars. It was a country on the go. The cold weather was a great propellant. You had to move to stay warm. I met Stuart and a few of his friends the next day and then headed back to the South of France.

Shelby had booked a two-week vacation in Sardinia, in an area called the Costa Smeralda, with my manager-lawyer and his wife Debbie. We brought a nanny along, Iris, a very sweet lady from Guatemala who we met in Los Angeles, to help Shelby with Gilbran and Paris. We also hired a Filipino couple, Nora and Domingo, to do the housework and some cooking. We really just needed Nora, but Domingo offered to work for nothing if he could stay in the garage as he had no other place to stay. Domingo was a sailor by trade, who was in between ships and was doing odd jobs around the neighborhood to help provide income for his family. He became Paris's body-guard and my boat valet while in Sardinia and a very trusted member of the Chong household.

The house we rented was right on the water and had every water toy imaginable from Lasers to jet skis to windsurfers. I tried windsurfing but kept losing my balance and falling into the water, which was warm and had an influx of jellyfish that stung like hell. Of course, I was in constant contact with those creepy little creatures and had the welts to prove it. I eventually settled on the two-person sailboat called a Laser. One day I found a deserted island about half a mile from our house that was clearly just used as a party spot given the debris scattered around. The little island was so beautiful that the junk piles looked obscene to me. So I made it my job to rid the place of all the garbage that littered the beach. Every day I spent a few hours cleaning and burying all the trash until it was spotless. It felt so good when I finished that I had a little celebration by myself on my little piece of paradise. The ocean around the Coast of Smeralda was almost too warm and pleasant. I spent many hours scuba diving and scraping sea urchin off the rocks to feed the little fish that would swarm around me as if I were their mother.

Shelby had purchased a Ferrari for my birthday and I had it shipped to Sardinia along with my Rolls Royce and Duechev (the French two-cylinder). We had no place to store our vehicles in the South of France so we just brought them with us wherever we went, along with eleven matching pieces of Louis Vuitton luggage. I had a ball driving my Ferrari in Sardinia with its winding roads and quaint little towns. I would attract a crowd whenever I drove it because I drove it so badly, mangling the gears every time I tried to look like I knew what I was doing.

I was happy with my life. I was a successful movie actor and director between films. I was with the love of my life and our children, having a vacation in one of the nicest places on the planet. I was on top of the world until I received a telephone call from my brother in Qualicum Beach, Canada, with news that my mother had died.

CHAPTER SEVENTEEN

STILL SMOKIN

Vancouver, British Columbia, Canada, 1982

My mother had been sick for some time, but she sounded very strong the last time I had talked to her. She even became quite animated and excited when I told her I was sending for her and Pop to visit us in the South of France. But she ended the conversation by telling me to take care of my brother. She had never told me that before. She was always telling my brother to take care of me when we were little, so it sounded a little strange at the time. And now I know that she was saying good-bye. She knew it was her time to go and she went. Just like that.

I went into shock and, after telling Shelby the news, I went out on the beach and cried like a baby. My dear, sweet, beautiful mother was gone forever. My mother, who could barely write because of her limited schooling (third grade), still wrote me letters every month. The letters were always full of love and understanding and gossip about the family. She was the one who would wake up when I came home and listen to my dreams of what I wanted to be no matter how crazy or far out they were. She was my protector and my friend but most of all she was my *mother*, who loved and worried about me. And now she was gone and I was sad. Shelby found me on the beach and held me in her arms, crying along with me. Together we mourned the woman who gave me life.

We flew back to Vancouver Island for the funeral and had a service in a little church down the road from their house. My dad was a total mess and I took him for a ride around Qualicum so he could talk to me about Mom. He wanted to talk about her, as if he could somehow bring her back by talking. Pop did not understand death. That sudden separation from someone with whom he had been for more than fifty years. It didn't make sense. Why was she not here? She was always here. Right in her favorite chair. In her bed. Her garden. Where was she?

My brother, Stan, told me that the day Mom died, Pop got into his car and drove a thousand miles back to Calgary where they had lived most of their lives, looking for her. He drove to the houses where they had raised us kids and tried to recapture the past. Then he drove the thousand miles back to the island hoping that she would be there to greet him when he returned, like she had greeted him before when he would come home from the road. My dad was a distance driver for Canadian Freightways and would be gone for days on end, but she was always there when he returned. Not this time.

After the service in Brower, Shelby and I returned to the motel were we were staying and tried to figure out our next move. The plan was to fly to Amsterdam to do *Still Smokin*, the concert movie, but first we would have to arrange for my friend Stuart to transport the Rolls, the Ferrari, and the Duechev to Amsterdam. As we were arranging to have Stuart, Domingo, and his friend drive the vehicles filled with the luggage back to Amsterdam, there was a knock on the door. I opened it to find two executives from Paramount movies standing there.

"Hi, Tommy! Well, it took some doing, but we found you!"

I stood there with my mouth open for a second and then invited them into the motel room.

"We chartered a plane in Seattle and here we are!"

"You rented a jet?" I replied.

"No, not a jet. It's just a Cessna but it got us here. Hey, sorry about your mom. We came because we heard you would be here for the funeral. We were ready to fly to Sardinia though . . ."

"In a Cessna?" I asked.

"Oh, no! We would need a jet for Sardinia."

"So, why did you come up? What's up?" I was dying to know the reason for their trip to the far north.

"We need a favor from you and Cheech. Cheech is already onboard. So now we need a favor from you. We are doing a movie, a spoof actually, about Hollywood. It's called *It Came from Hollywood* and we need you and Cheech to do a cameo. And like I said, Cheech is already onboard so . . ."

"Sure, I would be glad to be in your movie," I answered. I was still puzzled as to why they went through all this trouble.

The very next morning bright and early, we boarded the little Cessna and flew to Seattle, Washington, and then took a commercial flight to Los Angeles. The "we" being Jeffrey Katzenberg, Larry Marks, and me. Katzenberg was one of the top guns at Paramount at the time. The movie *It Came from Hollywood* was in trouble and needed some star power to put some butts in the seats. Cheech and Chong were the hottest movie stars at the time, so Jeffrey flew to Vancouver Island to get my support. Now I suppose he could have had an underling do the same job, but Jeffrey was a hands-on guy who would travel anywhere, anytime, if he felt it would sell tickets. This is why he went on to become cofounder and CEO of DreamWorks with Steven Spielberg and David Geffen. Years later, after Cheech and I had parted company, Katzenberg offered us parts in *The Lion King* for Disney. I have a ton of respect for Jeffrey; however, I did not want to work for Disney and I turned down the job. Of course, that was a very stupid thing to do, as *The Lion King* made a shitload of money for everyone involved. Cheech not only did the voice of Banzai the Hyena for *The Lion King*, but also other voice-over work and movies for anyone who would hire him. But I stand by my decision because I am a rebel and I take pride in being the guy who stayed true to the hippie code of peace, love, and good smoke.

Cheech and I shot our part in *It Came from Hollywood* in one afternoon, ad-libbing the entire shoot and having a ball with the rest of the celebrity cast—Dan Aykroyd, John Candy, and Gilda Radner among them. We got the go-ahead to shoot *Still Smokin* while I was in Hollywood, but Cheech still did not want to do the movie. Once we hired our favorite producer, Peter Macgregor-Scott, we got our money back and we were good to go.

We arrived in Amsterdam with my dad, Shelby, Paris, and Gilbran, and got rooms at the Akura Hotel. Domingo, my driver, had driven the cars from Sardinia with Stuart and had stories to tell about their trip. They had a couple of falling-outs along the way. Domingo told me that Stuart wanted to stop and party, pretending the Rolls and Ferrari belonged to him and that Domingo worked for him. Domingo told me that he came awfully close to stabbing Stuart with his knife. He even showed me his knife and where he was going to stab him if he did not do as he was told. I was in shock when I heard what an asshole Stuart had turned out to be. He was an opportunist and tried to take advantage of my trust, or rather, my stupidity. I was stupid to trust this guy without checking out his story first. But the angels take care of fools like me, which is why Domingo was there. He protected me and my belongings like a loyal friend.

I dropped Stuart immediately when I heard the horror stories from Domingo; however, I made a big mistake when I fired him before I got possession of my Rolls. The fucker stole my car. He had it stored in some friend's garage and would not tell me where it was until I paid him some money for the time he spent working on the film festival. Of course, he spent no time at all on anything except partying and pretending he was the owner of these fine automobiles. I was pissed, but I realized that he had me. I was too trusting and he had me. So I arranged for Joe Mannis, my L.A. lawyer-manager, to handle the problem. In other words, to pay the fucker and get back my Rolls. Cheech and Peter were getting huge laughs at my predicament; it was a typical, trusting Chong move that I was becoming famous for. Joe worked his magic and within a week I had my cars parked at the hotel.

Once the car problem was solved we started writing the movie. The plot was simple, as was to be expected. Cheech and Chong are invited over to the film festival by a shady producer who disappears with some money. The film festival people are Dutch and were led to believe that Burt Reynolds and Dolly Parton were coming. When we show up, they immediately think Cheech is Mr. Burt and I am Mr. Dolly. They take us to a hotel where we are given a suite with room service so we take full advantage of the opportunity . . . and the fun begins.

Once we started shooting the movie and watching dailies, Cheech and I clicked like we did in the old days. We got along fine as long as we were performing and creating. *Still Smokin* gave us a chance to put our live act on film, preserving our ten years of hard work forever. We performed the live part of the act in front of about one thousand people and filmed the show with multiple cameras, capturing the very last time we would perform live together. I will always remember that night because it was the end of a glorious career. We both had a strong feeling that it was the last time and when we held hands and took our last bow, I felt his grip squeeze a little tighter. And when we hugged, it lasted for a good moment. I was elated, happy, relieved, and exhausted. The comedy duo that started in Vancouver, Canada, with a young, fresh-faced American draft dodger and a Canadian Motown musician turned comic took its final bow in Amsterdam in front of a thousand adoring fans.

The concert footage was the last shot of the film and within days we were packed up and on our way back to Los Angeles, where I would be sitting with the editor and putting *Still Smokin* together. Peter found a little editing suite on Barham just a little way from the Hollywood Freeway. Editor James Coblentz was a young guy with a very hip sense of humor that meshed beautifully with the film.

Editors are so important to a film, which is why the good ones are always booked years ahead. This was one of the reasons I liked the young up-and-comers. They are usually available and will work ten times harder just to show the editing world that they are more than just assistants. The studio production head at Universal gave me a couple of pros when we were editing *Next Movie*, but they did not grasp the humor at all. They might have come around but I did not want to wait. Either you got it or you didn't. There was no in-between. Only the editors have the ability to see the movie that is buried inside the mishmash of scenes thrown together into a rough cut. Editors are like firemen who start a fire so they can put it out. With expertise, the editor snips here and moves this over there and discards that scene altogether, usually the director's favorite one. But when the movie starts to take form that favorite scene is totally forgotten, because in its place is a movie you forgot you were making.

The editor added his own touch into *Still Smokin*. The animals' fucking scene was James's stroke of genius. When Cheech and the German housekeeper make love, James cuts to animals fucking for effect. I loved it because it kept the movie funny without having to do reshoots, and the audience responded well to it. *Still Smokin* went on to gross forty or so million; Cheech and I have each made around ten million since its release. We picked the right title for the movie because even today it's *Still Smokin.*

While we were editing *Still Smokin,* Cheech told me that Mike Medavoy, the president of Orion Pictures, had pitched a sword-fighting movie to him. I immediately called Mike and had a meeting with him so I could hear the story right from the president's mouth. Howard Brown taught me to listen closely to whatever the president of a movie company wants you to do and the smart thing is to do it! By executing his idea, he is on the hook for the success of the movie, and will back it with the budget to ensure that it succeeds. So I listened and told him the truth—I loved it! Cheech and Chong as the Corsican Brothers! Perfect!

Cheech was less than enthusiastic for a couple of reasons when I told him. One, we had just finished a movie. And two, I was the director. I had tried to stop taking his objections to me directing personally, but it still bothered me. Actually, it pissed me off because once again I had to bring him into another project kicking and screaming, as if it were so terrible getting eight million in fees and a ten-million-dollar budget to do a comedy.

Cheech finally agreed to do the film on one condition—this movie would be dope free! No more pot jokes. Again, I felt like slapping the shit out of him. Pot is what made Cheech and Chong millions of dollars! Who else in the history of movies has made so much doing pot jokes? *No one, you pretentious little cocksucker!* I never said that but I sure thought it! But then the Gemini in me said, *Hey, what a great idea! Cheech and Chong being funny without pot jokes. Hey, I can do that!* So with the deal made, I headed back to the South of France to write the first draft of *The Corsican Brothers*.

The writing was fairly easy because the story was already written. I just had to tailor it to fit a Mexican and a half-breed Chinaman. I also made a casting decision that I knew would please Cheech. I hired Roy Dotrice, the famous English actor, to play the Evil Fuckaire (fucker). Roy suggested that we hire his wife Kay to play the woman who raises us. I also hired my daughters, Rae Dawn and Robbi, to act in the movie, along with Shelby and Rikki.

When the time came to do the location scouting, Peter Macgregor-Scott wanted us to shoot the entire film in Vienna, Austria, because of connections he had made on a previous film. I wanted to shoot in Paris, but to keep a happy camp I agreed to scout locations in Vienna. Location scouting is one of the more pleasant tasks one has in making a movie. You get to see parts of a city that nobody ever gets to see. We toured castles in Vienna where people actually lived and died in majestic splendor surrounded by unimaginable wealth, where the term "room temperature" for the wine meant twenty below zero. Some of those castles were fucking cold and dreary. I really did not want to shoot a movie being cold all the time, so I informed our producer that the movie would be shot in Paris. Cheech sided with Peter and preferred that the movie be shot in Vienna, but I was the director and I had final say. And that was that.

Shelby had been looking for a residence in Paris and found a beautiful apartment in the seventeenth district close to the Eiffel Tower. Our next-door neighbor was Mr. Masaru Ibuka, the guy who brought the transistor radio to the masses when he started a company called Sony. I had tea over at his flat one afternoon. He spoke no English and my Japanese was as bad as his English, but we got along famously. When he asked me if he could do anything for me, I asked him if he could get me a deal on a television set. I told him I prefer a Sony. He laughed hard at my request, but told his man to get me a good deal. I had met many great people in my time but meeting the man who changed the world like he did was probably the greatest honor ever. He was a kind and gentle man who loved to laugh.

The Corsican Brothers shoot was a dream. We used the same crew from Amsterdam with Harvey Harrison as the DP and scored a real sixteenth-century French château outside of Paris, where we shot the bulk of the film. We had six hundred acres to play with, plus a five-hundred-room castle with moats and forests and lakes around it. Everything was perfect. Too perfect. The meals for the cast and crew included wine at every meal and were served on tablecloth-covered tables under a tent beside the moat. You would think everyone would be happy with these conditions, right? Wrong.

The first ones to complain were the French actors. Actors in France pride themselves on being the best actors in the world for good reason. They can act. And they don't like standing around waiting. They need a script. They need to know who they are playing. They need to know the story. Some of them quit after the first day. But the ones who stayed were the actors who had worked without a script and could improv with the best of them.

Shelby and Rikki got to stretch out and do some real acting too. However, I had to dub over Rikki's voice with a voiceover expert to get the proper German accent for the part. Cheech disagreed with that decision and we had another falling-out over that one. Looking back, I don't think the voice change was necessary, but it was too late to do anything about it.

The execs at Orion were not thrilled that Cheech and Chong were making a dope-free movie on their dime and sent me a hash pipe as a reminder that dope was our trademark. But again, it was too late. We were moving along with the dope-free theme quite nicely, thank you. But I understood the movie company's concern, and in retrospect, it did hurt at the box office because the people stayed away in droves when the movie was released.

The tension between Cheech and Rikki was beginning to show. They were not getting along, mainly because Rikki had shipped her horses over to France and was riding every chance she got, preparing for the Olympics and shooting *The Corsican Brothers* at the same time. This left Cheech at home looking after their daughter, along with the help of a nanny, and Tacky, their crazy Australian sheepdog. Cheech was not a happy camper.

To make matters worse I wrote a scene that featured Shelby and me and asked Cheech to direct it for me. Cheech directed it like the pro that he is, but I could see that he saw the magic between Shelby and me—magic that he did not have with Rikki. Although, the funniest scene in *The Corsican Brothers* was when Cheech was washing Rikki's horse and hitting on her at the same time. As he talks he leans against the horse's rear and it looks like his arm is sucked into the horse's ass! Up to his shoulder. Cheech makes the face that tells you what is happening and when he pulls his arm out of the horse's ass, he is missing the brush. So he has to go in again to retrieve it. That, in my humble opinion, is the funniest scene in the movie.

The scene that I am most proud of is the last scene at

the castle where we follow my daughter Robbi, who plays the Queen's illegitimate black daughter, as she skips through the front door of the palace and out the back door to the grand party celebrating the end of the Evil Fuckaire at the end of the movie. The shot is one continuous take that goes steady without a cut for fifteen minutes. Good old Harvey designed that shot and it is genius.

The Corsican Brothers was a fun shoot and even though I spent all my lunch hours writing scenes, I was happy with everyone, especially the main cast of Edie McClurg and Roy and Kay Dotrice, who entertained us offscreen with games and stories and really helped me get through this epic intact with words of encouragement and love. It was a special thrill to work with my daughters: Rae Dawn, who played the Gypsy fortune teller in Paris, and my model daughter Robbi, who went on to star in the television show *Poltergeist* that was shot in Vancouver and ran for five years during the nineties. I put my dad in a scene that was cut out of the main print, but I have it somewhere. He looked so good in his French chef outfit.

The entire Chong and Marin family got to be in *The Corsican Brothers* and that was because I was the director. In the end it was worth all the arguments, fights, and discomfort that goes with making movies just to be able to put people you love in a major motion picture for all the world to see. I would not have had it any other way.

We edited *The Corsican Brothers* back in Los Angeles, using my regular editors Tom Avildsen and his crew. It was an easy edit because all the footage was there and then some. Not having the dope jokes turned the movie into a regular action-packed comedy adventure with weird Cheech and Chong humor. It worked on some levels, but it did not work for the stoner fans, who stayed away in droves. Orion Pictures declared bankruptcy soon after the release of *The Corsican Brothers* and went into receivership—whatever that means. Cheech and Chong also went into receivership because we never recovered from that last movie, either.

We worked together on *After Hours*, the Martin Scorsese–directed vehicle that was a nice art house hit. We played a couple of thieves who were terrorizing the neighborhood and being hunted down by vigilantes. And we also appeared in *Yellowbeard*, a movie written by and starring the Monty Python people. This was another mercy fuck for Cheech and Chong, who were written in for their audience appeal rather than for their humor.

I moved back to Paris and spent a good deal of my time caring for Gilbran and Paris. Precious was attending a very exclusive private school in Switzerland with other kids of famous and rich parents. Shelby was studying French and enjoying Paris. Rikki had filed for divorce and left Malibu for Pennsylvania. And Cheech met an artist named Patti Heid and brought her to Paris so we could work on a new comedy album.

I was not into the album at all, but I liked working with Cheech and it was fun reliving the recording days. The bits were a bit strained and not as current as the other albums, but Cheech was intent on making this album. He wrote words to a Bruce Springsteen song "Born in the U.S.A.," changing it to "Born in East L.A." He never left anything for me to do in the song like I always did for him, so it was his and his alone. He called me when they were recording it and wanted me to come down and sing background on the tune. I felt insulted. Every fucking tune that we did together I made sure he sang lead if I wrote the lyrics and I always included him, except for in *Up in Smoke*.

That's right. I wrote that one for me alone and he added the Mexican part. I considered myself a filmmaker, but when

Cheech wanted to do a video of the tunes we wrote, like "Get Out of My Room," I told him to direct it himself. After all, it was his vision. So he did. He not only directed it, but also kept my part to a minimum—again, pissing me off!

The record was released to a very ho-hum response and that was that. In the meantime I received an offer to direct a couple of comics in a movie called *Dumb Dicks*. Lorin Dreyfuss, Richard's brother, and David Landsburg had written a script, sold the movie to Cannon Pictures, and were looking for a director. I agreed to direct it for half a million dollars. We were to shoot in Rome and I was to leave immediately. I stopped off in Paris to pick up my son Paris and off we went to Rome to location scout.

The scouting part was great because we had access to all the great sites in Rome. We were taken to places in the Colosseum that no tourist had ever been to before. They took us to a sunken city outside of Rome where they had full-size replicas of famous Roman battles reenacted with slaves and gladiators fighting one another to the death. I was taken to the oldest garbage dump on the planet. This ancient dump is now a solidified mountain that was once all the garbage of Rome. I walked on the Appian Way where the Romans once crucified Christians— one every hundred yards for twenty miles! This ancient road is littered with shards of pottery and marble and is still in better shape than 90 percent of the roads in America.

I had glanced at the script on the flight over to Rome and was ready to get down and make it shootable. The guys had written a lot of scenes for themselves, but there was no love story. The film needed a reason for people to stay in the theaters and watch. Something! Nothing happened. It was just a series of so-called funny things strung together that did not make me interested in watching it. So I met with Lorin and David and tried to convey my thoughts and concerns. They listened politely but were not the least bit concerned. But I am a comic. I know when something is not funny. And this movie was not funny.

Then it hit me. They think it's funny! This is their version of funny, not mine. I knew what I had to do. I had to take myself out of the picture. They did not need me there fucking up their vision. They needed to direct this movie themselves. So I told them as their director my first job was to fire myself. I gathered up my son, went back to Paris, and then flew back to Los Angeles, where I met with Menahem Golan and gave him back the two hundred and fifty thousand dollars and told him I could not help this movie. Menahem looked at me for a long time. Not too many people in the movie business give money back, but I had not earned it and I would not feel right about keeping what is not mine. He thanked me for being honest with him, and a few years later told me I was smart leaving the movie. It died at the screening and never made it to theaters.

A couple of weeks later, I was relaxing at my home in Bel Air when I received a call from Cheech, asking if he could stop by because he had something to tell me. It had been a while since we had spoken to each other and I was looking forward to seeing my old partner. I immediately sensed something was wrong when he walked into the house and sat down. I waited for him to tell me what was up and after a long pause he said, "I have been offered a movie and I am going to take it."

I don't think I said anything but my head was pounding. The blood had rushed to my head and I felt like I was going to pass out.

Cheech went on. "Columbia wants me to do *Born in East L.A.* And I am going to do it. You took that movie in Rome, so . . ."

"I was hired to direct the movie and I pulled out before they started shooting . . ." I was talking but my mind was somewhere else. I looked into Cheech's eyes and he looked away. He got up to leave. "So that's it?" I said. Did I say it or was I thinking it? My mind was racing now. My heart was pounding. I felt like I was drowning.

"What about the act?" I asked. "It's all yours," he replied.

Cheech walked to his car and then he turned and said, "I still want to do Cheech and Chong. But I am going to do this movie by myself . . ."

I don't think I answered because he got into his car and drove off. I stood outside my Bel Air house for a long time. I was mad. I was so mad because I knew it was over and I didn't want it to be over. I wanted it to go on and on until we were old men. I wanted to make funny movies for the rest of my life with Cheech because we had something that no one else had. We had honesty. Our humor came from the gut. It was real, every joke we did had truth to it. Our movies rang with so much truth that you had to watch them over and over to get every little nuance, every little movement, because they captured real-life experiences. We influenced the entire planet, first with our records, then with the movies. We have had entire generations after generations watch and study our movies to learn the culture of the sixties. We carried the sixties into the seventies, the eighties, the nineties, right up to the present time. And we did it with six albums, six movies, and ten years of personal appearances. Richard Marin and Tommy Chong. Cheech and Chong.

Cheech went on to write and direct *Born in East L.A.* and he called me to do a cameo in his movie, but I refused. It was another insult. A fucking cameo. I stayed away from *Born in East L.A.* because I knew it would only piss me off. And I was right. When I finally saw his movie I did get pissed off because it was a lie. He did exactly what I would never let him get away with: He acted the part. He became a Hollywood actor playing different characters. Like we really need more fucking actors in Hollywood.

I tried to stay true to myself. I took a couple of minor roles and I turned down a shitload of television work, including *Nash Bridges* because they wanted me to play a cop. I wrote scripts instead. I would spend months working on scripts and then make halfhearted attempts to sell them. I did take the role of Leo on *That '70s Show* because I loved the title. I was the seventies and the part was written for me. It took a while to get into the television groove but I did it and I enjoyed every minute of the five seasons that I appeared on that show. I would sit and watch Dave Trainer teach the kids how do act for television. I learned how to take the writer's words and make them my own. And I learned the joys of rehearsals. Cheech and I rarely rehearsed. In fact, we never rehearsed. We just went out and did it.

In 1991, six years after the breakup, I spent New Year's Eve with Dennis Miller, the comedian from *Saturday Night Live*, who was in Vancouver visiting his wife's parents. We chatted for a while and Dennis told me he had a gig at the local comedy club in Gas Town. I told him I wanted to come and see him perform, so he left tickets for me at the door. I arrived just as he was about to go on and visited him in the dressing room. He was pacing around the room getting ready for his show and he said, "Do you still get nervous before you go on?" I laughed because it had been years since I performed. Since I was always with Cheech I don't think we ever got nervous, because there were two of us.

Dennis went on and I thought his show was great. I wanted to do that. I wanted to get back onstage and do stand-up. So I got my five minutes together and did a show in the Valley the night after Rodney King got his ass beat by the cops. My bit had to do with the mothers of the cops talking to one another, bragging about their sons being on television. About halfway through my act I got heckled. A guy yelled, "Hey, where's Cheech?" That comment threw the act into a question and answer period about Cheech and Chong, a pattern that would follow me wherever I performed.

A week or so later I signed up to perform at The Laugh Factory on Sunset. I went on and did my five minutes and just as I got off the stage, Sam Kinison walked into the club with his girlfriend and a few other people. Sam was about the hottest comic on the scene at this time and his entrance created quite a buzz with the rest of the audience.

"Chong, you're a comic god!" With that statement Sam kneeled down on one knee and kissed my hand.

I was embarrassed. I had just stumbled through a five-minute routine and now one of the greatest comics in the world was kneeling before me kissing my hand. The other comics who had taken the stage were having a hard time competing for the audience's attention with all this going on in the background, so Jamie Masada, the owner of the club, escorted the gang of us upstairs to his private office. Once in the office, Sam and his guys lit up a big stinky joint and passed it around. I was thrilled being in the presence of this great comic and I acted like a fan. Sam felt the same about me and he was acting like a fan. It was a mutual admiration society for the hour or two we spent together.

Sam talked to me as if he had known me for years. He told me how he was influenced by the Cheech and Chong records. He talked about how he got into comedy through his preaching and healing in the name of the Lord. I told him how I first saw him doing a set at the Comedy Store at two in the morning and how fucking funny he was even at that late hour. The talk on the town was that Mitzi, the wild-haired owner and mother of Pauly Shore, would not let Sam perform earlier because no one could follow him. He was so wild and crazy and his material was so off the wall and sometimes downright disgusting that two AM was the only time they would let the beast out of his cage.

I loved Sam. He was a by-product of Cheech and Chong with his Lenny Bruce/Richard Pryor attitude onstage. And watching Sam made me proud to be a comedian. We did a couple of gigs together, notably a New Year's special with me, Sam, and Pauly Shore in Vegas. Sam wanted to hook up with me and do a tour he called "Screech and Chong." I was waiting for the gig to materialize when Sam was killed by a drunk driver. I was being driven to a comedy gig in New Jersey when the driver gave me the news of Sam's death.

When I got offered to do a gig in Guam and Palau, a couple of islands off the coast of Japan, I jumped at the chance to combine work with a little pleasure and asked my lady to join me. Shelby politely declined, as she had declined all my other pleadings to join me on the road because I hated going out there alone. The Guam gig was the final straw though, and when she declined, I gave her an offer she couldn't refuse. I asked her to be in the show. Shelby had been studying acting and had appeared in a few B movies, notably the Troma Horror Films, but was struggling like the millions of beautiful talented actresses in Hollywood. My offer came at the right time because now she could perform and be with me at the same time, so she accepted my offer.

Her first time onstage was in Guam, where she introduced me and then introduced a couple of my characters, like Hairy Palms, the world's masturbation champion, and Blind Melon

Chitlin', the great blues singer. She loved the thrill of being in front of a live audience and has been my comedy partner now for more than ten years. She replaced Cheech in more ways than just onstage. We share the fun of being comedians.

Comedy is like rock climbing. It's tough and the higher you get, the higher your chance of serious injury if you make one mistake. You have to know what you are doing and it isn't for everyone. Listen to Donald Trump when he tells you "never give up." If you want to be a comic, then be a comic. There is no shortcut. It is all hard work. I mean, you have to work maybe fifteen or twenty minutes when you first start! And that is only one show. Add two shows and that's forty minutes of stage time. And the rest of the day is spent looking for material, which means watching television, going to movies, or working at Starbucks. It's hard work being a comic, make no mistake about it! (That's a quote from George W. Bush.) It's hard work, especially if you like to eat, drink, and party all night. Because there is nothing to stop you.

When people ask me who my favorite comic is, I tell them they are all my favorites. Even the ones who borrow material from other comics. I feel a good joke is like a joint. It tastes better when it is shared with others.

So that's my story and I am sticking to it. I left out Cheech's career after me because that's his story and he should tell it. There is a happy ending, however. The Cheech and Chong story isn't over. Not by a long shot.

We appeared together in 2005 at the Aspen Comedy Festival, making it almost twenty years since our last time together onstage. We both had flown in on separate private jets with his arriving in Aspen before mine. I was very excited about this affair because it was a comedy festival and I assumed that we were going to be doing some Cheech and Chong comedy. I had talked briefly with Cheech before flying in and told him what bits we could do. He did not want to do any bits, but he listened to me—as he always did in the past—and I thought it was settled. I told him we could do Harry and Margaret because this was a bit where Cheech had no lines. No dialogue whatsoever. All he had to do was get an old lady's dress and wig, which I offered to get for him, but he protested and said he would pick up his own costume. I assumed that he would because Cheech had always taken a lot of care picking out the right costumes for the bits. But when we finally met in his room, he told me that he did not want to do any comedy. Not Harry and Margaret, nothing! He just wanted to sing a Chuck Berry song with the band that was there for Fred Willard.

I had to go along with his plan, but I did persuade him to do one Cheech and Chong song, "Mexican Americans." He could not refuse that request because he wrote it and sang it in *Next Movie*. I had another reason for asking him to sing "Mexican Americans"—I was planning to answer his song with one that I wrote while he was singing his song. That song was "Beaners."

We rehearsed with Fred Willard's band and later that night we performed both songs. But before we performed we had a question-and-answer session with a moderator. Cheech was wearing the suit he wore in *Nash Bridges* and was very straight and dry in answering the questions. This was not the wisecracking Chicano I had been partners with for fifteen years. No, not at all. I sat there and interrupted Cheech, correcting him on many points about our career, and soon my correcting him became a bit! Cheech would say something and I would say, "Uh, no, man, that's not how it happened." I could see he was getting a little frustrated trying to deal with the stoner I had turned into, but hey, just because Cheech went straight didn't mean I had to fake it! Someone asked him how difficult it was to change his "Chicano stoner image," and he replied, "It was like turning a big ship around." The moderator then asked me the same question and I answered, "I didn't have to turn my ship around because it was going in the right direction." Cheech quit comedy to become a serious actor, while I struggled in comedy club learning the art of stand-up.

Our performance was the next night, and true to his plan, Cheech sang his Chuck Berry song and then went into "Mexican Americans," leaving me room to come in with "Beaners." Cheech had not heard my updated version of the tune so he had a few laughs at rehearsal, but the night of the show he was not laughing because I went on to sing a version of "Me and My Old Lady" that I would do in my live show. It went something like "Me and my old lady, we like we like, we like to come to Aspen, Colorado, and rent a Cheech and Chong tape. Go home and make some popcorn, then smoke a real big fat one, get so stoned you forget you got the tape! So you end up watching the Discovery Channel, some show about two frogs fucking. You start thinking 'Gee, Cheech looks funny without his mustache, and who's that frog fucking him? It looks like Don Johnson!' Then you find the tape a month later, bring it back, and pay a hundred dollars!"

That song used to kill at the comedy clubs all across America and it killed at Aspen. They told me Cheech was pacing back and forth like a caged animal when I did that song. He was pissed and did not talk to me the rest of the time in Aspen. We tried to have a "meeting" with some agents who wanted to pitch us a tour idea, but Cheech was not into getting back together, not after what he went through. I felt great because I got off! And in comedy "getting off" is the goal. When you get off you feel so good for the rest of the night. And I felt great that night.

We ended up in Bob Gersh's Aspen house, where I was surrounded by industry people wanting to talk business. I ended up making a book deal with my editor from Simon & Schuster, who loved my Don Johnson song. And this is the second book with those crazy S&S girls. When I got the book deal in Aspen my life changed dramatically because all of a sudden I had to write a book. By myself.

It was a struggle, but I had a good deal of it written already. This is how I spent quality time in the joint. Writing! The book was called *The I Chong* and it made a few bestseller lists, notably *The New York Times*, and it sold a respectable amount of copies. I'm hoping that this one goes through the roof; not everyone knows about my stint in the clink, but everyone knows Cheech and Chong. Our story will never die completely because we have left too many reminders around during our fifteen-year career. The record collection is still selling units. The movies are still being rented. And now the story of Cheech and Chong will live on forever in this book.

THE CHEECH AND ME

Los Angeles, California, March, 2008

People often ask me if Cheech and I are ever going to get back together, and I have always had a hard time answering that question. Until now.

Back in February 2005 at the Aspen Comedy Festival, my agent, Matt Blake, offered Cheech a deal to do a Cheech and Chong reunion tour with me at various two-thousand-seat theaters across America. When he had a negative reaction to the idea and refused to discuss it further, I knew there was little hope of reviving the old act. But I respected his decision and moved on.

Not long ago, I was putting the finishing touches on this book when I got a call from his new manager, Ben Feigin, inviting me out to Cheech's house in Malibu. The supposed purpose of the meeting was for Cheech to present me with an offer—an offer that turned out to be the exact same deal he turned down three years earlier in Aspen. While I was still open to the idea of a reunion tour, I knew we couldn't do our old act because I saw how resistant he was to doing those bits the last time we were onstage together. I could not trust him, and the one thing needed in a comedy act is trust. You have to be sure that the other guy is going to "show up" at the gigs. And when Cheech failed to "show up" in Aspen, it was evident he did not want to be Pedro or Margaret or any of the old characters.

However, I did figure out a way for us to reunite as Cheech and Chong without doing the old act—and that was with music. Music could save us . . . or at least be the foundation for creating a new show. We had enough tunes in our library to do a tour that consisted entirely of music. We had "Earache My Eye," "Basketball Jones," "Bloat On," "Black Lassie," "Going Downtown," plus a list of songs that I had written for my solo act. My plan was to hold auditions for the rest of the band and record the process on tape. It would be almost like a Cheech and Chong–*American Idol* reality show—*Cheech and Chong: The Musical*. It seemed like a foolproof idea that couldn't possibly fail because we could play music venues and large festivals without any of the difficulties involved in performing stand-up in places better suited for musical acts. The only thing I insisted on was that we had to perform the tunes in character so as to distance ourselves from *Duets,* where Cheech appeared as himself and failed to impress the judges.

I was feeling good about our future because my idea made sense and it was so doable. However, when I presented the idea to Cheech he became irate.

"Why don't you want to do the old act?" he asked.

"Well, I don't know, I thought the music angle was originally your idea and . . ."

He cut me off. "Don't try that one . . . My idea! Yeah, right! People don't want to see us doing music! They want to see us doing comedy. Sometimes you come up with some good ideas, Chong, but this isn't one of them."

As Cheech went on his angry rant—which degenerated into a bitter discussion about who wrote what movie and how lousy my book *The I Chong* was—I felt that he had lost his comedy chops. Cheech had been performing in comedy clubs with a troupe of Spanish comics as the emcee, and according to my spies, his act consisted of exactly what I was suggesting. The only difference was that he was doing music in comedy clubs and was not performing in character. Audiences don't come to comedy clubs to hear music like that, so the reaction was less than enthusiastic. Of course, I didn't come to that realization until I was in my car driving home.

As I listened to Cheech insult my ability as a writer I realized I could no longer work with the guy. He had changed. He had become The Cheech. He had a line of acting credits way longer than mine and would not allow me to steer the "career boat" like I did in the beginning. He had grown out of my grasp and had become another person—a person with whom I could no longer relate. There was a time when we could feel each other's moods and know exactly what the other person was thinking. But that time was gone forever. And so was the Cheech I knew and loved.

I sat and listened to this stranger for an hour and a half before I finally had had enough and decided to leave.

As I got ready to go he said, "So what do you think about the tour offer?"

I replied, "I don't think so, man. The money is nice, but I don't need the money."

He looked at me and sneered, "That's not what I heard."

"Really? What did you hear?"

"I heard that you could really use the money."

I smiled to myself and thought, *Hey, I'm still married to the same woman for over twenty years! I haven't been through two divorces like you, and I'm happy . . .* I thought it but I didn't say it. I think I said something like, "Yeah, well, I am making enough to pay the bills and that's all I really need."

To tell you the truth, I don't really know what I said in that moment. I was still in shock. Cheech said such mean things to me about my book *The I Chong*—he accused me of using a ghost writer (which doesn't really make sense. If he thought the writing was so bad, wouldn't it be more insulting to say he could tell I wrote it myself?), and he also said that the book got the worst reviews ever in the history of books! No matter how many compliments you get, the only comments that stick in your mind are the nasty ones.

When I got home and recounted my meeting with Cheech to Shelby, as usual, she had the right insight: "You guys should name your next movie *Grumpy Old Stoners* because that's what you two have become."

I thought, *Wow*, Grumpy Old Stoners. *Yeah! I like that. I think I'll start writing that as soon as I finish this book.*

Oh, hey, guess what? It looks like I'm finished.

ACKNOWLEDGMENTS

There are so many people to acknowledge that I am afraid it will take another book. I will try to just list the important people who may or may not have made it into the book, but were very instrumental in the success of Cheech and Chong.

The first person, of course, is my beautiful soulmate/comedy partner/wife, Shelby. She was there in the beginning and she was there at the end. My daughters, Precious, Robbi, and Rae Dawn, who supplied me with jokes for the records and ideas and performances for the movies. My sons Paris and Gilbran and my grandsons Morgan and Jack. This male energy helped me remain macho during this whole writing experience.

I have to thank Rikki for her stories and support. And Patti Marin for her support and stories about The Cheech. Both ladies gave me a glimpse into the private life of my old partner and for that I will always be in their debt. I have to give a big shout-out to Jimmy Root, who, although he was not in the book, deserved the award given to the Best Damn Roadie in comedy. Jimmy supplied us with ideas to improve the act (sound effects) that were so innovative that we used them in the movies. Jimmy deserves a book all about Jimmy because he performed beyond the call of duty many, many times.

I want to thank Peter Macgregor-Scott, our unit manager for *Next Movie*, *Still Smokin*, and *The Corsican Brothers*. Peter gave me a crash course in filmmaking that saved our asses many, many times. I want to thank Oscar and Elsie, Cheech's parents, for raising such a talented guy. And I want to give a shout-out to Cheech's sisters, cousins, and other relatives for providing us with so much material. And a special shout-out to Cheech's children, Carmen, Joey, Jasmine, and the little grandson.

I want to thank Evelyn and Pat Morita for their support when I went to jail and when we shot the movies. Pee-wee Herman (a.k.a. Paul Reubens) gets a hug and a salute for helping us make a funny movie even funnier. The gang at the Groundlings deserves a big round of appreciation for their help in supplying us with the most talented actors in Hollywood. Bob Stane, the owner of the Ice House, deserves a smile and a pat on the butt for helping Cheech and me perfect our act by being just one of three clubs that actually paid us to perform—and the Ice House always paid the best back then.

I have to acknowledge the crews on the movies, who also helped this first-time director in so many ways. The sound guys would remind me where I was in the script and what I needed to make the scene work. My script supervisors would spend their lunch breaks writing the additional dialogue into the script so as not to mess up the editors. I have to thank Howard Brown for giving me a career as a director and Eric Wooster for introducing video assist into the C&C movies. A special hug to Kay Dotrice for being our mom during the shooting of *The Corsican Brothers*. Howard, Eric, and Kay have since passed away, but they will be remembered forever on the pages of this book.

I would not be allowed to live in the U.S.A. if I did not acknowledge my manager and friend during the heyday, Joe Mannis. Joe and his wife, Debbie Mannis, produced *The Corsican Brothers* and *Still Smokin*, while their son Seth became a fine artist. Stan Coleman and Eric Wiessman, the genius lawyers who helped us during the movie years, also deserve a shout-out. And the guy who made it all happen deserves a big hello and thank-you as well. Mr. Lou Adler and Ode Records were hip enough to see what we were doing, and they helped make it happen. Lou's cousin, Marshall Blonstein, the head of sales at Ode, also introduced me to Howard Brown, who made The Cheech and The Chong millions of dollars. And a mention to Howard Franks, Lou's assistant, who is still dealing with *Up in Smoke* thirty-five years later. And thanks to Ryan Tracy for keeping Cheech and Chong alive with his site during the years when there was no Cheech and Chong.

A big hug and shout-out to Trish, the genius who is editing this heap of writing. Thank you, Trish . . . thank you, thank you, thank you . . .

And last, I want to thank The Cheech, for without him there would be no Cheech and Chong and therefore no story to tell . . . so thank you, Cheech, and good luck with your golf game.